AA POCK

PORT

Contents

English edition prepared by First Edition Translations Ltd, Great Britain

Designed and produced by AA Publishing

First published in 1995 as Wat & Hoe Portugees,
© Uitgeverij Kosmos bv - Utrecht/Antwerpen

Van Dale Lexicografie bv - Utrecht/Antwerpen

This edition © The Automobile Association 1997

Reprinted May 1999
Reprinted Feb and Sep 2000
Reprinted May 2001
Reprinted Aug 2002

A CIP catalogue record for this book is available from the
British Library

ISBN: 0 7495 1475 2

Published by AA Publishing (a trading name of Automobile Association
Developments Limited, whose registered office is Millstream,
Maidenhead Road, Windsor, Berkshire SL4 5GD.
Registered number 1878835)

Typeset by Anton Graphics Ltd, Andover, Hampshire.

Printed and bound by G. Canale C.SpA, Torino, Italy.

Photocredits for front cover: Cockerels of Barcelos, Spectrum Colour
Library; woman in traditional dress, Images Colour Library; Torre de
Belem, Lisbon, Zefa Pictures Ltd

Find out more about AA Publishing and the wide range of services the
AA provides by visiting our web site at www.theAA.com

Introduction

● **Welcome to the AA's new Essential Phrase Books series, covering the most popular European languages and containing everything you'd expect from a comprehensive language series. They're concise, accessible and easy to understand, and you'll find them indispensable on your trip abroad.**

Each guide is divided into 15 themed sections and starts with a pronunciation table which gives you the phonetic spelling to all the words and phrases you'll need to know for your trip, while at the back of the book is an extensive word list and grammar guide which will help you construct basic sentences in your chosen language.

Throughout the book you'll come across coloured boxes with a 🖐 beside them. These are designed to help you if you can't understand what your listener is saying to you. Hand the book over to them and encourage them to point to the appropriate answer to the question you are asking.

Other coloured boxes in the book - this time without the symbol - give alphabetical listings of themed words with their English translations beside them.

For extra clarity, we have put all English words and phrases in black, foreign language terms in red and their phonetic pronunciation in italic.

This phrase book covers all subjects you are likely to come across during the course of your visit, from reserving a room for the night to ordering food and drink at a restaurant and what to do if your car breaks down or you lose your traveller's cheques and money. With over 2,000 commonly used words and essential phrases at your fingertips you can rest assured that you will be able to get by in all situations, so let the Essential Phrase Book become your passport to a secure and enjoyable trip!

Pronunciation table

English speakers can imitate the actual sound of the words by saying the version in italics. Correctly placed stress is essential:
Words ending in a vowel or in **m** or **s** are usually stressed on the penultimate syllable, for example:

    o rato   *(oo rah-too)*   the mouse

Words that end in a consonant other than **m** or **s** are stressed on the last syllable e.g. ***cruel*** *(croo-ell)* - cruel, and exceptions to the rule are words marked with an accent, for example, ***falência*** (bankruptcy). Emphasised nasal pronunciation is indicated by the til accent (~), for example, ***nações*** *(nations)*.

Vowels

ã	pronounced approximately as in **sung** (*irmã*)
ão	pronounced as **ow** in **howl** (*limão*)
final **e**	barely pronounced (*onde*)
ê	as in **they** (*relê*)
es	*sh* as in **Estoril** (*shtooreel*)
final **o**	as in **loop** (*macaco*)
ô	as in **local** (*vôo*)
u	as in **rule**, and silent in *gue, gui, que* and *qui*

Consonants

ç	as in **receive**, e.g. *laço*
ch	as in **shock**, e.g. *choque*
h	always silent, e.g. *hora*
lh	as **ll** in **million**, e.g. *milhão*
nh	as **ni** in **onion**, e.g. *linha*
qu	before **e** or **i** pronounced as in **kick**, e.g. *quilo*; before **a** or **o** pronounced as in **quote**, e.g. *qualidade*
r	always trilled
-s-	before **b, d, g, l, m, n, r** and **v**, as in **leisure** e.g. *rasgo*
-s-, -s	before **c, f, p, qu, t** and when it is the last letter, with a **sh** sound as in **sugar**, e.g. *respeito*
x	initial or before a consonant as pronounced as in **sugar**, e.g. *xícara*; in **ex** pronounced as in **squeeze**, e.g. *exemplo*
z	when in final position, as in **leisure**, e.g. *conduz*, otherwise like an ordinary z

Useful lists

What day is it today?	Que dia é hoje?
	kuh deeah eh oarje?
Today's Monday	Hoje é segunda-feira
	oarje eh segunda-fayrah
– Tuesday	Hoje é terça-feira
	oarje eh tearsah-fayrah
– Wednesday	Hoje é quarta-feira
	oarje eh cuartah-fayrah
– Thursday	Hoje é quinta-feira
	oarje eh keentah-fayrah
– Friday	Hoje é sexta-feira
	oarje eh seshtah-fayrah
– Saturday	Hoje é sábado
	oarje eh sarbadoo
– Sunday	Hoje é domingo
	oarje eh doomeengoo
in January	em Janeiro
	ey janayroo
since February	desde Fevereiro
	desduh fevverayroo
in spring	na primavera
	nuh preemaverrah
in summer	no verão
	noo verau
in autumn	no outono
	noo ohtohnoo
in winter	no inverno
	noo invairnoo
1997	mil novecentos e noventa e sete
	meel novsentush ee nooventa ee set
the twentieth century	o século XX (vinte)
	oo seckooloo veent
What's the date today?	Que dia é hoje?
	kuh deeah eh oarje
Today's the 24th	Hoje é dia vinte e quatro
	oarje eh deeah veent ee cuartroo
Monday, November 2nd, 1998	segunda feira, dois de Novembro de 1998
	segunda fayrah, doysh duh novembroo duh meel novsentush ee novventa ee aytoo
in the morning	de manhã
	duh manyair
in the afternoon	de tarde
	duh tard
in the evening	à noite
	ah noyt
at night	de noite
	duh noyt
this morning	hoje de manhã
	oarje duh manyair
this afternoon	hoje à tarde
	oarje ah tard

this evening _____	hoje à noite
	oarje ah noyt
tonight _____	esta noite
	eshta noyt
last night _____	na noite passada
	nah noyt passada
this week _____	esta semana
	eshta semarnah
next month _____	no próximo mês
	noo prossimoo mayge
last year _____	no ano passado
	noo arnoo passardoo
next... _____	no próximo...
	noo prosseemoo...
in...days/weeks/ _____	daqui a...dias/semanas/meses/anos
months/years	*dakee ah...deeash/semarnash/mayzesh/*
	arnoosh
...weeks ago _____	há...semanas
	ah...semarnash
day off _____	feriado
	ferriardoo

1.2 Bank holidays

● **The main public holidays** in Portugal are the following:

January 1	Ano Novo (New Year's Day)
February	Carnaval (Carnival)
March/ April	Sexta-feira Santa (Good Friday)
April 25	Dia da Revolução (Day of the Revolution)
May 1	Dia do Trabalhador (Labour Day)
June 10	Dia de Portugal (Camões Day commemorating Portugal's equivalent to Shakespeare)
June 13	Santo António (Festival of St. Anthony, patron saint of Lisbon)
June 24	São João (Festival of St. John, celebrated in Oporto and the North)
August 15	Assunção da Nossa Senhora (Feast of the Assumption)
October 5	Dia da República (Republic Day)
November 1	Dia de Todos os Santos (All Saints Day)
December 1	Restauração da Independência (Restoration Day)
December 8	Imaculada Conceição (Feast of the Immaculate Conception)
December 25	Dio da Nata (Christmas Day)

Most shops, banks and government departments are closed on these days.
Boxing Day is not a public holiday.

1.3 What time is it?

What time is it? _____	Que horas são?
	kay oarash sow?
It's nine o'clock _____	São nove horas
	sow nov oarash
– five past ten _____	São dez e cinco
	sow dez ee seenkoo

Useful lists

– a quarter past eleven	São onze e um quarto	*sow onz ee oom cuartoo*
– twenty past twelve	É meio dia e vinte	*eh mayoo deeah ee veent*
– half past one	É uma e meia	*eh oomah ee mayah*
– twenty-five to three	São três menos vinte e cinco	*sow trayge mennush veent ee seenkoo*
– a quarter to four	São quatro menos um quarto	*sow cuartroo mennush oom cuartoo*
– ten to five	São cinco menos dez	*sow seenkoo mennush dej/*
– twelve noon	É meio dia	*eh mayoo deeah*
– midnight	É meia noite	*eh mayah noyt*
half an hour	uma meia hora	*oomah mayah orah*
What time?	A que horas?	*ah kay orash?*
What time can I come round?	A que horas é que posso ir?	*ah kay orash eh kuh possoo eer?*
At...	Às...	*ush...*
After...	Depois das...	*depoysh dush...*
Before...	Antes das...	*antesh dush...*
Between...and...	Entre as...e as...	*entrash...ee ush...*
From...to...	Das...às...	*dush...ush*
In...minutes	Daqui a...minutos	*dakee uh...minootoosh*
– an hour	Daqui a uma hora	*dakee uh ooma ora*
– ...hours	Daqui a...horas	*dakee uh...orash*
– a quarter of an hour	Daqui a um quarto de hora	*dakee ah oom cuartoo dora*
– three quarters of an hour	Daqui a três quartos de hora	*dakee ah trayge cuartoosh dora*
early/late	cedo/tarde	*sedoo/tard*
on time	a horas	*uh orash*
summertime	horário de verão	*oraryoo duh verau*
wintertime	horário de inverno	*orarioo duh invairnoo*

1.4 One, two, three...

0	zero	*zairoo*	
1	um	*oom*	
2	dois	*doysh*	
3	três	*trayge*	

4		quatro	*cuartroo*
5		cinco	*seenkoo*
6		seis	*saysh*
7		sete	*set*
8		oito	*oytoo*
9		nove	*nov*
10		dez	*dej*
11		onze	*onz*
12		doze	*doaze*
13		treze	*treyze*
14		catorze	*cattorz*
15		quinze	*keenze*
16		dezasseis	*dezzasaysh*
17		dezassete	*dezzaset*
18		dezoito	*dezzoytoo*
19		dezanove	*dezzanov*
20		vinte	*veent*
21		vinte e um	*veenty oom*
22		vinte e dois	*veenty doysh*
30		trinta	*treenta*
31		trinta e um	*treenty oom*
32		trinta e dois	*treenty doysh*
40		quarenta	*cuarenta*
50		cinquenta	*seencuenta*
60		sessenta	*sessenta*
70		setenta	*settenta*
80		oitenta	*oytenta*
90		noventa	*nooventa*
100		cem	*same*
101		cento e um	*sentoo ee oom*
110		cento e dez	*sentoo ee dej*
120		cento e vinte	*sentoo ee veent*
200		duzentos	*doozentoosh*
300		trezentos	*trayzentoosh*
400		quatrocentos	*cuartroosentoosh*
500		quinhentos	*keenyentush*
600		seiscentos	*sayshsentoosh*
700		setecentos	*setsentoosh*
800		oitocentos	*oytsentoosh*
900		novecentos	*novsentoosh*
1000		mil	*meel*
1100		mil e cem	*meely same*
2000		dois mil	*doysh meel*
10,000		dez mil	*dej meel*
100,000		cem mil	*say meel*
1,000,000		milhão	*meelyau*
1st		primeiro	*preemayroo*
2nd		segundo	*seggoondoo*
3rd		terceiro	*tairsayroo*
4th		quarto	*cuartoo*
5th		quinto	*keentoo*
6th		sexto	*seshtoo*
7th		sétimo	*settimoo*
8th		oitavo	*oytahvoo*
9th		nono	*nohnoo*
10th		décimo	*dessimoo*

11th _____	décimo primeiro	*dessimoo preemayroo*
12th _____	décimo segundo	*dessimoo segundoo*
13th _____	décimo terceiro	*dessimoo tairsayroo*
14th _____	décimo quarto	*dessimoo cuartoo*
15th _____	décimo quinto	*dessimoo keentoo*
16th _____	décimo sexto	*dessimoo seshtoo*
17th _____	décimo sétimo	*dessimoo settimoo*
18th _____	décimo oitavo	*dessimoo oytarvoo*
19th _____	décimo nono	*dessimoo nohnoo*
20th _____	vigésimo	*veejezimoo*
21st _____	vigésimo primeiro	*veejezimoo preemayroo*
22nd _____	vigésimo segundo	*veejezimoo segoondoo*
30th _____	trigésimo	*treejezimoo*
100th _____	centésimo	*sentezimoo*
1000th _____	milésimo	*milezimoo*

once _____	uma vez	*ooma vayzh*
twice _____	duas vezes	*dooash vayzesh*
double _____	o dobro	*oo dobroo*
triple _____	o triplo	*oo treeploo*
half _____	a metade	*uh mettard*
a quarter _____	um quarto	*oom cuartoo*
a third _____	um terço	*oom tairsoo*
a couple, a few, some ____	um par de, uns, alguns	*oom par duh, oonsh, algoomash*
2+4=6 _____	dois mais quatro são seis	*doysh mysh cuartroo sow saysh*
4-2=2 _____	quatro menos dois são dois	*cuartroo mennush doysh sow doysh*
2x4=8 _____	dois vezes quatro são oito	*dooash vayzesh cuartroo sow oytoo*
4÷2=2 _____	quatro a dividir por dois são dois	*cuartroo uh divvideer por doysh sow doysh*
odd/even _____	par/ímpar	*par/eempar*
total _____	(em) total	*(aim) tootal*
6x9 _____	seis por nove	*saysh por nov*

🔴 .5 The weather

Is the weather going to be good/bad?	Estará bom/mau tempo? *estarah bom tempoo?*
Is it going to get colder/hotter?	Estará mais frio/calor? *estarah mysh freeooh/calore?*
What temperature is it going to be?	Quantos graus vão estar? *cuarntoosh growsh vow eshtar?*
Is it going to rain?	Vai chover? *vy shoover?*

Is there going to be a ____ storm?	Vamos ter uma tempestade? *varmoosh ter ooma tempeshtard?*
Is it going to snow? ____	Vai nevar? *vy nevvar?*
Is it going to freeze? ____	Vai haver nevoeiro? *vy aver nevvooayroo?*
Is the thaw setting in? ____	Vai fazer trovoada? *vy fazzair troovooarda?*
Is it going to be foggy? ____	O tempo vai mudar? *oo tempoo vy moodar?*
It's cooling down ____	Vai arrefecer *vy arryfessair*
What's the weather ____ going to be like today/ tomorrow?	Que tempo vamos ter hoje/amanhã? *kuh tempoo varmoosh tair oarje/ahmanyar?*

abafado muggy	fresco cool	quente hot
aguaceiro shower	frio cold	quentíssimo scorching hot
ameno mild	gelo ice	rajadas de vento squalls
bom tempo fine	geada frost	ruim bleak
céu limpo clear	granizo hail	tempestuoso stormy
céu pouco/muito nublado	... graus abaixo/ acima de zero	trovoada thunderstorm
light/heavy clouds	...degrees above/ below zero	vaga de calor heatwave
(cheio de) sol sunny	húmido damp	vento wind
chuva rain	nebuloso cloudy	vento fraco/ moderado/forte
chuvisco drizzle	neve snow	light/moderate/ strong wind
chuvoso wet	nevoeiro fog	ventoso windy
ciclone hurricane	nublado overcast	

 .6 Here, there...

See also 5.1 Asking for directions

here/there ____	aqui/ali *akee/alee*
somewhere/nowhere ____	em algum/nenhum lugar *aim algoom/nenewm loogar*
everywhere ____	em todo o lado *aim tohdoo oo lardoo*
far away/nearby ____	longe/perto *lonj/peartoo*
right/left ____	para a direita/esquerda *parra uh dirrayta/eshkerda*

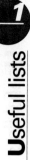

1

Useful lists

right/left of _____	à direita/esquerda de
	ah dirrayta/eshkerda duh
straight ahead _____	em frente
	aim frent
via _____	por
	poor
in _____	em
	aim
on _____	sobre
	sohbre
under _____	debaixo de
	debyshoo duh
against _____	contra
	contrah
opposite _____	em frente
	aim frent
next to _____	ao lado de
	ow lardoo duh
near _____	perto
	pairto
in front of _____	em frente de
	aim frent duh
in the centre _____	no centro
	noo sentroo
forward _____	para diante
	parra deeant
downward _____	para baixo
	parra byshoo
upward _____	para cima
	parra seema
inward _____	para dentro
	parra dentroo
outward _____	para fora
	parra foura
backward _____	para trás
	parra traj
at the front _____	à frente
	ah frent
at the back _____	atrás
	atraj
in the north _____	no norte
	noo nort
to the south _____	para o sul
	para oo sool
from the west _____	de oeste/do oeste
	di esht/doo esti
from the east _____	de leste/do leste
	duh lesht/doo lesti
to...from _____	a...de
	ah...duh

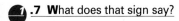

.7 What does that sign say?

See also 5.4 Traffic signs

aberto/fechado **open/closed**	escada rolante **escalator**	proibido fazer fogueira **no open fires**
água não potável **not drinking water**	homens **gents/gentlemen**	proibido fotografar **no photographs**
alta tensão **high voltage**	horário **opening hours**	proibido fumar **no smoking**
aluga-se **for hire**	informações **information**	proibido pisar a relva **keep off the grass**
avariado/não funciona **out of order**	lavabos **toilets**	propriedade privada **private (property)**
caixa **pay here**	liquidação **clearance**	recepção **reception**
completo **full**	liquidação total closing-down **sale**	reservado **reserved**
cuidado com o cão **beware of the dog**	não mexer **do not touch**	saída **exit**
cuidado com o degrau **mind the step**	passagem/ entrada proibida **no entry**	saída de emergência **emergency exit**
é favor não incomodar **do not disturb**	perigo **danger**	saldos **sale**
elevador **lift**	perigo de incêndio **fire hazard**	senhoras **ladies**
empurre/puxe **push/pull**	posto de primeiros socorros **first aid**	sinal de alarme **alarm signal**
escada **steps**	primeiro andar **first floor**	tinta fresca **wet paint**
entrada **entrance**	proibida a entrada de animais **no pets allowed**	vende-se **for sale**
entrada livre/ grátis **entry free**		
escada de incêndio **fire escape**		

.8 Telephone alphabet

a _____	*ah*	América	*amereeka*
b _____	*bay*	Bernardo	*bairnardoo*
c _____	*say*	Colónia	*colonnia*
d _____	*day*	Dinamarca	*deenamarca*
e _____	*eh*	Espanha	*eshpanya*
f _____	*ef*	França	*fransa*
g _____	*jey*	Grécia	*gressia*
h _____	*gar*	Holanda	*ollanda*
i _____	*ee*	Irlanda	*earlanda*
j _____	*jotta*	Japão	*japown*
k _____	*kappa*	Kremlim	*kremleen*
l _____	*el*	Londres	*londresh*
m _____	*me*	Madrid	*madree*
n _____	*ene*	Nápoles	*napolesh*
o _____	*oh*	Oslo	*ojloo*

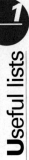
p_____	*peh*	Portugal	*poortoogarl*
q_____	*q*	Quilo	*keeloo*
r_____	*err*	Rússia	*roossia*
s_____	*ess*	Suécia	*swessia*
t_____	*tay*	Turquia	*toorkeea*
u_____	*u*	Uruguai	*ooroogwy*
v_____	*vay*	Vitória	*veetoria*
w_____	*vay*	Washington	*vasheengton*
x_____	*sheej*	Xangai	*shangai*
y_____	*ípsilon*		
z_____	*zey*	Zurique	*zooreek*

1.9 Personal details

surname_____	apelido	
	apelleedoo	
christian name(s)_____	nome	
	nom	
initials_____	iniciais	
	iniciaish	
address (street/number) ___	morada (rua/número)	
	moorada (rua/noomeroo)	
post code/town _____	código postal	
	coddigoo pooshtal	
sex (male/female) _____	sexo (masculino/feminino)	
	sexoo (mashculeenoo/ femineenoo)	
nationality _____	nacionalidade	
	nasseeonalidad	
date of birth _____	data de nascimento	
	data duh nashsimentoo	
place of birth _____	local de nascimento	
	local duh nashsimentoo	
occupation_____	profissão	
	proofissow	
married/single/divorced____	casado/solteiro/divorciado	
	cazadoo/solltayroo/divorciadoo	
widowed _____	viúva/viúvo	
	vioova/vioovoo	
(number of) children _____	(número de) filhos	
	noomeroo duh feelyoosh	
identity card/passport/_____	número de bilhete de identidade/	
driving licence number	passaporte/carta de condução	
	noomeroo duh beelyet duh eedentidad/	
	passaport/carta duh condusow	
place and date of issue ____	local e data de emissão	
	loocal ee data duh emissow	

Courtesies

2 Courtesies

● **It is usual in Portugal** to shake hands on meeting and parting company. Female friends and relatives may kiss each other on both cheeks when meeting and parting company. With men this varies according to the region.

2 .1 Greetings

Hello, Mr Smith _____	Olá, senhor Smith/Olá, Seu Smith
	olah,senyor Smith/olah sayoo Smith
Hello, Mrs Jones _____	Olá, Senhora Jones
	olah, senyora Jones
Hello, Peter _____	Olá, Peter
	olah, Peter
Hi, Helen _____	Viva, Helen
	viva, Helen
Good morning, madam____	Bom dia, minha senhora
	bom deeah, meenya senyora
Good afternoon, sir _____	Boa tarde, senhor
	Boa tard, senyor
Good evening_____	boa noite
	boa noyt
Good day_____	Bom dia
	bom deeah
How are you? _____	Como está?
	comoo eshtah?
Fine, thank you, _____ and you?	Bem obrigado, e o senhor?
	baim obrigahdoo, ee oo senyor?
Very well _____	Óptimo
	otimoo
Not very well _____	Mais ou menos
	maiz oh mennush
Not too bad_____	Vai se andando
	vysuh andandoo
I'd better be going_____	Vou andando
	vo andandoo
I have to be going. _____ Someone's waiting for me	Tenho de ir. Estão à minha espera
	tenyo duh ear. eshtau uh meenya eshperah
Goodbye _____	Tchau!
	chau
See you soon _____	Adeus!
	adayoosh!
See you later _____	Até logo!
	atay loggoo!
See you in a little while____	Até breve!
	atay brev!
Sleep well _____	Durma bem
	dourma baim
Goodnight_____	Boa noite
	boa noyt
All the best _____	Que tudo lhe corra bem
	kuh toodoo lher courrah baim
Have fun_____	Divirta-se
	deeverts suh

Good luck	Muita sorte/Boa sorte
	muinta sort
Have a nice holiday	Boas férias
	boash ferriash
Have a good trip	Boa viagem
	boa viarjaim
Thank you, you too	Obrigado, igualmente
	obbrigahdoo, eeguarlment
Say hello to...for me	Dê cumprimentos a...
	day coomprimentoosh ah...

2 .2 How to ask a question

Who?	Quem?
	kaim?
Who's that?	Quem é?
	kaim eh?
What?	O quê?
	oo kay?
What's there to see here?	O que é que se pode visitar aqui?
	oo kee eh kuh suh pod veesitar akee?
What kind of hotel is this?	Que tipo de hotel é este?
	kuh teepoo di ohtel eh esht?
Where?	Onde?
	ond?
Where's the toilet?	Onde são os lavabos?
	ond sow oosh lavarboosh?
Where are you going?	Para onde vai?
	parra ond vy?
Where are you from?	De onde é?
	di ond eh?
How?	Como?
	commoo?
How far is that?	A que distância fica?
	ah kay dishtancia feeka?
How long does that take?	Quanto tempo dura?
	cuarntoo tempoo doura?
How long is the trip?	Quanto tempo dura a viagem?
	cuarntoo tempoo doura ah veeargaim?
How much?	Quanto?
	cuarntoo?
How much is this?	Quanto custa isto?
	cuarntoo cooshter eeshtoo?
What time is it?	Que horas são?
	kay orash sow?
Which?	Qual? Quais?
	quarl? cwysh?
Which glass is mine?	Qual é o meu copo?
	quarl eh oo mayoo coppoo?
When?	Quando?
	cwarndoo?
When are you leaving?	Quando é que parte?
	cwarndoo eh kuh part?
Why?	Porquê?
	poorkay?
Could you...me?	Poderia...me?
	pooderia...muh?

Could you help me, please?	Poderia ajudar-me se faz favor?
	pooderia ajoodar muh suh faj favor?
Could you point that out to me?	Poderia indicar-mo?
	pooderia eendi-eecar moo?
Could you come with me, please?	Poderia vir comigo, se faz favor?
	pooderia veer comeego, suh faj favor?
Could you reserve some tickets for me, please?	Poderia reservar-me bilhetes?
	pooderia resairvar muh beelyettsh?
Do you know whether...?	Por acaso, sabe se...?
	por acarzoo, sab si...?
Do you have...?	Tem...?
	tame...?
Do you know another hotel, please?	Conhece outro hotel?
	koonyes ohtroo ohtel?
Could you give me...?	Podia dar-me...?
	poodeeah dar muh...?
Do you have a vegetarian dish, please?	Tem por acaso um prato sem carne?
	tame poor acasoo oom prartoo same carn?
I'd like...	Eu queria...
	ew kereeah...
I'd like a kilo of apples, please.	Eu queria um quilo de maçãs
	ew kereeah oom keeloo duh massangsh
Can I...?	Posso...?
	possoo...?
Can I take this?	Posso levar isto?
	possoo levvar eeshtoo?
Can I smoke here?	Posso fumar aqui?
	possoo foomar akee?
Could I ask you something?	Posso fazer-lhe uma pergunta?
	possoo fazzair lhuh ooma pairgoontah?

2.3 How to reply

Yes, of course	Sim, claro
	see, claroo
No, I'm sorry	Não, desculpe
	now, deshcoolp
Yes, what can I do for you?	Em que posso ser-lhe útil?
	aim kuh possoo sair lheh ooteel?
Just a moment, please	Um momento, se faz favor
	oom moomentoo, suh fash favvor
No, I don't have time now	Não, agora não tenho tempo
	now, agorah now tenyoo tempoo
No, that's impossible	Não, isso é impossível
	now, eessoo eh imposseevel
I think so	Creio que sim
	crayoo kuh see
I agree	Eu também penso que sim
	eyoo tambaim pensoo kuh see
I hope so too	Também o espero
	tambaim oo eshpearoo
No, not at all	Não, de modo nenhum
	now, duh mohdoo nenyoom
No, no one	Não, ninguém
	now, ningame
No, nothing	Não, nada
	now, narda

That's (not) right	Isso está certo (isso está errado) *eesoo eshtah sairtoo (eesoo eshtah errardoo)*
I (don't) agree	(Não) estou de acordo/Não concordo consigo *(now) eshtoe di acordoo/now concordoo conseegoo*
All right	Está certo *eshtah sairtoo*
Okay	De acordo *di acordoo*
Perhaps	Talvez *talvayj*
I don't know	Não sei *now say*

.4 Thank you

Thank you	Obrigado/muito obrigado *obbrigahdoo/mweentoo obbrigahdoo*
You're welcome	De nada/foi um prazer *duh narda/foy oom prahzair*
Thank you very much	Muitíssimo obrigado *mweenteessimoo obbrigahdoo*
Very kind of you	Muito amável da sua parte *mweentoo amarvel da suah part*
I enjoyed it very much	Foi um verdadeiro prazer *foy oom verdadayroo prahzair*
Thank you for your trouble	Agradeço-lhe o incómodo *agraddaysoo lhyer oo eencomodoo*
You shouldn't have	Não precisava se incomodar *now preceesarva si eencomoodar*
That's all right	Não tem de que *now taim duh kay*

.5 Sorry

Sorry!	Perdão *perdow*
Excuse me	Com licença *com leesensa*
I'm sorry!	Desculpe! *deshcoolp!*
I'm sorry, I didn't know...	Desculpe, eu não sabia que ... *deshcoolp, eyoo now sabeeah kuh...*
I do apologise	Desculpe-me *deshcoolp muh*
I'm sorry	Lamento *lamentoo*
I didn't do it on purpose, it was an accident	Não fiz de propósito, foi sem querer *now feej duh propozeetoo, foy same kerrair*
That's all right	Não faz mal *now faj mal*
Never mind	Deixe lá *daysh la*
It could've happened to anyone	Pode acontecer com toda a gente *pod acontessair com toeda ah jent*

.6 What do you think?

What do you think?	O que acha?
	oo keh asha?
What do you prefer?	O que prefere?
	oo keh prefair?
Don't you like dancing?	Não gosta de dançar?
	now goshta duh dansar?
I don't mind	É me indiferente/ Tanto faz
	eh muh eendeeferent/ tantoo faj
Well done!	Muito bem!
	mueentoo baim!
Not bad!	Não está mal!
	now eshtah mal!
Great!	Optimo!
	ottimoo!
Wonderful!	Que delícia!
	kay delleecia!
It's really nice here!	Que bem que se está aqui!
	kay baim kuh si eshtah akee!
How nice!	Que giro/bonito!
	kay geeroo/ booneetoo!
How nice for you!	Que bom para si!
	kay bom parra see!
I'm (not) very happy with...	(Não) estou muito contente com...
	(now) eshtoe mweentoo content com...
I'm glad...	Alegra-me que ...
	allegra muh kuh...
I'm having a great time	Divirto-me muito
	deeveertoo muh mweentoo
I'm looking forward to it	Aguardo com muito prazer ...
	agwardoo com mweentoo prazair...
I hope it'll work out	Espero que dê resultado
	eshpairoo kuh day resultardoo
That's ridiculous!	Que ridículo!
	kay reedeecooloo!
That's terrible!	Que terrível!
	kay tereevel!
What a pity!	Que pena!
	kay pena!
That's filthy!	Que sujo!
	kay soojoo!
What a load of rubbish!	Que disparate!
	kay deeshparatt!
I don't like...	Não gosto de ...
	now goshtoo duh
I'm bored to death	Aborreço-me terrívelmente
	aboressoo muh terreevelment
I've had enough	Estou farto/farta
	eshtoe fartoo/ farta
This is no good	Assim não pode ser
	assee now pod sair
I was expecting something completely different	Esperava outra coisa completamente diferente
	eshperarvah ohtra coyza completament deeferent

Courtesies

22

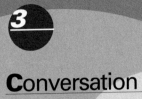

Conversation

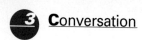

Conversation

Conversation

3

.1 I beg your pardon?

I don't speak any/ _____ I speak a little...	Não falo/falo um pouco *now faloo/faloo oom poocoo*
I'm English _____	Sou inglês/inglesa *so inglej/ingleza*
I'm Scottish_____	Sou escocês/escocesa *so eshcossayj/eshcossayza*
I'm Irish _____	Sou irlandês/irlandesa *so earlandayj/earlandayza*
I'm Welsh_____	Sou galês/sou galesa *so gallayj/so gallayza*
Do you speak _____ English/French/German?	Fala inglês/francês/alemão? *fala inglej/fransayj/allaymau?*
Is there anyone who_____ speaks...?	Há alguém que fale...? *ah algaim kuh fal...?*
I beg your pardon? _____	O que é que diz? *oo kay eh kuh deej?*
I (don't) understand _____	(Não) compreendo *(now)comprayendoo*
Do you understand me? ___	Compreende-me? *comprend muh?*
Could you repeat that, ____ please?	Podia repetir se faz favor? *poodeer repeteer suh faj favvor?*
Could you speak more_____ slowly, please?	Podia falar mais devagar? *poodeer falar mysh de-vaggar?*
What does that word _____ mean?	O que significa aquilo/aquela palavra? *oo kuh signifeeka akeeloo/akella pallavra?*
Is that similar to/the _____ same as...?	É (quase) a mesma coisa que...? *eh (quaz) ah mejma coyza kuh...?*
Could you write that_____ down for me, please?	Podia escrever? *poodeer eshcrevair?*
Could you spell that _____ for me, please?	Podia soletrar? *poodeer soolittrar?*
(See 1.8 Telephone alphabet)	
Could you point that_____ out in this phrase book, please?	Podia indicar aqui no guia? *poodeer indeecar akee noo gueea?*
One moment, please,_____ I have to look it up	Um momento, tenho de procurar *oom moomentoo tenyoo duh procurar*
I can't find the word/the ___ sentence	Não encontro a palavra/a frase *now encontroo ah palarvra/ ah frarz*
How do you say_____ that in...?	Como é que se diz em ...? *cohmoo eh kuh suh deej aim...?*
How do you pronounce_____ that?	Como é que se pronuncia? *cohmoo eh kuh suh proonoonsia?*

May I introduce myself? ___	Posso apresentar-me? *possoo apprezentar muh?*
My name's... ___	Chamo-me... *shamoo muh...*
I'm... ___	Sou... *so...*
What's your name? ___	Como se chama? *commoo suh shamma?*
May I introduce...? ___	Apresento lhe... *aprezentoo lhya...*
– my wife/ daughter/___ mother/girlfriend	A minha mulher/filha/mãe/amiga *uh meenya moolyer/feelya/ameega*
– my husband/son/___ father/boyfriend	O meu marido/filho/pai/amigo *oo mayoo mareedoo/feelyoo/ameegoo*
How do you do ___	Muito prazer em conhecê-lo *mueentoo prazair aim coonyessay loo*
Pleased to meet you___	Muito prazer (em conhecê-lo) *mueentoo prazair aim coonyessay loo*
Where are you from? ___	Donde é?/De onde é? *dond eh?/di ondi eh?*
I'm from ___ England/Scotland/Ireland/ Wales	Sou da Inglaterra/Escócia/Irlanda/Gales *so da eenglatera/eshcossia/eerlanda/garlesh*
What city do you live in?___	Em que cidade mora? *aim kay sidard mora?*
In... It's near... ___	Em... É perto de... *aim... eh pairtoo duh*
Have you been here ___ long?	Já está cá há muito tempo? *jah eshtah cah hah mweentoo tempoo?*
A few days ___	Há uns dias *ha unsh deeash*
How long are you ___ staying here?	Quanto tempo fica cá? *cuarntoo tempoo feeka cah?*
We're (probably) leaving___ tomorrow/in two weeks	Partimos (provavelmente) amanhã/daqui a duas semanas *partimoosh (proovarvelment) armanyar/dakee ah dooash semarnash*
Where are you staying?___	Onde está hospedado? *ond eshtah oshpedardoo?*
In a hotel/an apartment ___	Num hotel/apartamento *noom ohtel/ apartarmentoo*
On a camp site ___	Num parque de campismo *noom park duh campeejmoo*
With friends/relatives ___	Em casa de uns amigos/familiares *aim carza di uns amigoosh/familiaresh*
Are you here on your ___ own/with your family?	Está cá sozinho/com a família? *eshtah cah sozeenyoo/com ah fameelya?*
I'm on my own___	Estou sozinho *eshtoe sozeenyoo*
I'm with my ___ partner/wife/husband	Estou com a minha amiga/o meu amigo/a minha mulher/o meu marido *eshtoe com ah meenya ameega/oo mayoo ameegoo/ah meenya mullyer/oo mayoo mareedoo*

Conversation

25

– with my family	Estou com a minha família
	eshtoe com ah meenya fameelya
– with relatives	Estou com familiares
	eshtoe com familiaresh
– with a friend/friends	Estou com um amigo/uma amiga/amigos
	eshtoe com oom ameegoo/ooma ameega/ameegoosh
Are you married?	É casado/casada?
	eh cazardo/cazarda
Do you have a steady boyfriend/girlfriend?	Tens namorado/namorada?
	taynsh namorardoo/namorardah?
That's none of your business	Não tem nada com isso
	now taim narda com eesoo
I'm married	Sou casado/casada
	so cazardo/cazarda
– single	Sou solteiro/solteira
	so soltayroo/soltayrah
– separated	Estou separado/separada
	eshtoe separardoo/separardah
– divorced	Estou divorciado/divorciada
	eshtoe deevorciardoo/deevorciardah
– a widow/widower	Sou viúva/viúvo
	so veeoova/veeoovoo
I live alone/with someone	Vivo sozinho/com um companheiro
	veevoo sozzeenyoo/com oom companyayroo
Do you have any children/grandchildren?	Tem filhos/netos?
	taim feelyoosh/nettoosh?
How old are you?	Que idade tem?
	kuh eedad taim?
How old is she/he?	Que idade tem ela/ele?
	kuh eedad taim ella/el?
I'm...	Tenho...anos
	tenyo...anoosh
She's/he's...	Ela/ele tem...anos
	ella/el taim...anoosh
What do you do for a living?	O que é que faz?
	oo kay eh kuh faj?
I work in an office	Trabalho num escritório
	trabalyoo noom eshcritoryoo
I'm a student/ I'm at school	Estudo/ando na escola
	eshtoodoo/andoo nah eshcolla
I'm unemployed	Estou desempregado
	eshtoe dezempregardoo
I'm retired	Estou reformado
	eshtoe refformardoo
I'm on a disability pension	Estou reformado por causa de inválidez
	eshtoe refformardoo por cowza di eenvallidesh
I'm a housewife	Sou dona de casa
	so donna duh carza
Do you like your job?	Gosta do seu trabalho?
	goshta doo sayoo trabalyoo?
Most of the time	Às vezes sim, às vezes não
	aj vaizesh see, aj vaizesh now
I usually do, but I prefer holidays	Geralmente sim, mas gosto mais de férias
	jerarlment si maj goshtoo mysh duh ferriash

3 .3 Starting/ending a conversation

Could I ask you something?	Posso fazer-lhe uma pergunta? *possoo fazer lyer ooma pergoontah*
Excuse me	Desculpe *deshcoolp*
Excuse me, could you help me?	Desculpe, podia ajudar-me? *deshcoolp poodeer ajoodar muh?*
Yes, what's the problem?	Sim, o que é? *see oo kee eh?*
What can I do for you?	O que deseja? *oo kuh dezayjah?*
Sorry, I don't have time now	Desculpe, agora não tenho tempo *deshcoolp agorah now tenyoo tempoo*
Do you have a light?	Tem lume? *taim loom?*
May I join you?	Posso sentar-me ao seu lado? *possoo sentar muh ow sayoo lardoo?*
Could you take a picture of me/us? Press this button	Podia tirar-me/tirar-nos uma fotografia? Carregue neste botão. *podia tirrar muh/tirrar nooz ooma fotgrafffia? carreg nesht bootau*
Leave me alone	Deixe-me em paz *daysh muh aim paj*
Get lost	Vá-se embora! *vah suh emborah!*
Go away or I'll scream	Se não se for embora, começo a gritar! *suh now suh for emborah comessoo ah greetarr!*

3 .4 Congratulations and condolences

Happy birthday/many happy returns	Feliz aniversário! *feleej annivaisaryoo!*
Please accept my condolences	Os meus pêsames *oosh mayoosh pezamesh*
I'm very sorry for you	Sinto muito *seentoo mueentoo*

3 .5 A chat about the weather

See also 1.5 The weather

It's so hot/cold today!	Que calor/frio está hoje! *kay calorr/freeyoo eshtah oarje!*
Nice weather, isn't it?	Que bom tempo! *kay bom tempoo!*
What a wind/storm!	Que vento/tempestade! *kay ventoo/tempeshtad!*
All that rain/snow!	Que chuva/neve! *kay choova/nev!*
All that fog!	Que nevoeiro! *kay nevooayroo!*
Has the weather been like this for long here?	O tempo já está assim há muitos dias? *oo tempoo jah eshtah aseem ah mueentoosh deeash?*

Conversation

Is it always this hot/cold ___ here?	Aqui está sempre tanto calor/frio?
	akee eshtah semprah tantoo calor/freeyoo?
Is it always this dry/wet ___ here?	Aqui o tempo está sempre tão seco/húmido?
	akee oo tempoo eshtah semprah tau saycoo/ oomidoo?

.6 Hobbies

Do you have any _____ hobbies?	Tem algum passatempo?
	taim algoom passatempoo?
I like painting/_____ reading/photography/ DIY	Gosto de pintar/ler/fotografar/biscates
	gostoo duh peentar/lair/fotoggrafar/ beeshcatsh
I like music _____	Gosto de música
	goshtoo duh moosica
I like playing the _____ guitar/piano	Gosto de tocar guitarra/piano
	goshtoo duh toocar guitarra/ pianoo
I like going to the movies __	Gosto de ir ao cinema
	goshtoo duh ir ow cinaymah
I like travelling/_____ sport/fishing/walking	Gosto de viajar/fazer desporto/pescar/passear
	goshtoo duh veeajar/fazair deshportoo/passeear

.7 Being the host(ess)

See also 4 Eating out

Can I offer you a drink? ____	Posso oferecer-lhe uma bebida?
	possoo offeressair lya ooma bebbeeda?
What would you like_____ to drink?	O que é que queres beber?
	oo kee eh kuh cairesh bebbair?
Something non-alcoholic,__ please	Preferia uma bebida não alcoólica
	prefferia ooma bebbeeda now alcoohollica
Would you like a _____ cigarette/cigar/to roll your own?	Quer um cigarro/charuto/cigarro de enrolar?
	care oom cigaroo/sharootoo/cigaroo duh enroolar?
I don't smoke _____	Não fumo
	now foomoo

.8 Invitations

Are you doing anything____ tonight?	Vais fazer alguma coisa esta noite?
	vysh fazzair algooma coyza eshta noyt?
Do you have any plans ____ for today/this afternoon/tonight?	Já tem planos para hoje/esta tarde/hoje à noite?
	jah taim planoosh parra oarje/eshta tard/ oarje ah noyt?
Would you like to go _____ out with me?	Gostaria de sair comigo?
	goshtareeah duh syeer commeegoo?
Would you like to go _____ dancing with me?	Quer dançar comigo?
	care dansar commeegoo?
Would you like to have ____ lunch/dinner with me?	Quer almoçar/jantar comigo?
	care almoosar/jantar commeegoo?

Would you like to come to the beach with me?	Quer ir à praia comigo?
	care eer ah prya commeegoo?
Would you like to come into town with us?	Quer ir ao centro connosco?
	care eer ow sentroo conoshcoo?
Would you like to come and see some friends with us?	Quer ir a casa de uns amigos connosco?
	care eer ah carza di unsh ameegoosh conoshcoo?
Shall we dance?	Vamos dançar?
	varmoosh dansar?
– sit at the bar?	Vámonos sentar no bar?
	vamoo noosh sentar noo bar?
– get something to drink?	Vámos beber qualquer coisa?
	varmoosh bebbair qualcair coyza?
– go for a walk/drive?	Vámos dar uma volta a pé/de carro?
	varmoosh dar ooma vollta ah peh/duh cahroo?
Yes, all right	Sim, está bem
	si eshtah baim
Good idea	Boa idéia
	boa eedaya
No (thank you)	Não (obrigado)
	now obrigardoo
Maybe later	Talvez logo
	talvej loggoo
I don't feel like it	Não me apetece
	now muh aptess
I don't have time	Não tenho tempo
	now tenyoo tempoo
I already have a date	Já tenho outro encontro
	jah tenyoo ohtroo encontroo
I'm not very good at dancing/volleyball/swimming	Não sei dançar/jogar voleibol/nadar
	now say dansar/joogar volleybol/naddar

3.9 Paying a compliment

You look wonderful!	Estás com tão bom aspecto!
	eshtash com tau bom ashpectoo!
I like your car!	Que lindo carro!
	kuh leendoo cahroo!
You have beautiful hair	Tens cabelo lindo!
	tensh cabayloo leendoo!
You're a nice boy/girl	És um rapaz amoroso/uma rapariga amorosa
	ez oom rappaj amorozzo/ooma rappareega amorozza
What a sweet child!	Que criança amorosa!
	kay creeansa amorozza!
You're a wonderful dancer!	Danças muito bem!
	dansash mweentoo baim!
You're a wonderful cook!	Cozinhas muito bem!
	coozeenyash mweentoo baim!
You're a terrific soccer player!	Jogas futebol muito bem!
	joggash footboll mweentoo baim!

3.10 Chatting someone up

I like being with you _____ Gosto de estar contigo
goshtoo di eshtar conteegoo

I've missed you so much __ Senti muito a tua falta
sentee mweentoo ah tooah falta

I dreamt about you _____ Sonhei contigo
sonyay conteegoo

I think about you all day ___ Penso o dia inteiro em ti
pensoo oo deeah eentayroo aim tee

You have such a sweet _____ Tens um sorriso lindo
smile *taynz oom sooreesoo leendoo*

You have such beautiful ___ Tens uns olhos tão lindos
eyes *taynz oonz ollyoosh tau leendoosh*

I'm in love with you _____ Estou apaixonado/a por ti
eshtoe appaishonardoo/a por tee

I'm in love with you too __ E eu por ti
ee ew por tee

I love you _____ Amo-te
ammoo tuh

I love you too _____ Eu também te amo
ew taubaim tee ammoo

I don't feel as strongly _____ Não sinto um grande amor por ti
about you *now oo seentoo oom grand amor por tee*

I already have a _____ Já tenho um namorado/uma namorada
boyfriend/girlfriend *jah tenyoo oom namorardoo/ooma namorardah*

I'm not ready for that _____ Ainda não cheguei a esse ponto
ayeenda now shegay ah ess pontoo

This is going too fast _____ Eu preciso de mais tempo
for me *ew preseeezoo duh mysh tempoo*

Take your hands off me ____ Não te metas comigo
nao tuh metash commeegoo

Okay, no problem _____ Está bem, não faz mal
estah baim now faj mal

Will you stay with me _____ Ficas esta noite comigo?
tonight? *feecash eshtah noyt commeegoo?*

I'd like to go to bed_____ Quero ir para a cama contigo
with you *keroo eer parra ah camma conteegoo*

Only if we use a condom __ Só com um preservativo
soh com oom preservateevoo

We have to be careful _____ Temos de ser cautelosos com a SIDA
about AIDS *taymoosh de sair cowtellozush com ah seeda*

That's what they all say____ É o que todos dizem
eh oo kuh toedoosh deezaim

We shouldn't take any _____ Não podemos correr riscos
risks *now poodaymoosh correr reeshcush*

Do you have a condom? __ Tens um preservativo?
taynz oom preservateevoo?

No? In that case we _____ Não? Então não podemos
won't do it *now? entau now poodaymoosh*

3.11 Arrangements

When will I see you again?	Quando é que te volto a ver?/Quando é que vejo você de novo? *cwarndoo eh kuh tuh voltoo ah vair?*
Are you free over the weekend?	Tem tempo no fim-de-semana? *taim tempoo noo feem duh semarna?*
What shall we arrange?	O que é que combinamos? *oo ki eh kuh combinarmoosh?*
Where shall we meet?	Onde nos encontramos? *one nuz encontrarmoosh?*
Will you pick me/us up?	Vem buscar-me/nos? *vaim booshcar muh/noosh?*
Shall I pick you up?	Posso ir buscálo/la? *possoo eer bushcar loo/la?*
I have to be home by...	Tenho de estar em casa às... *tenyoo di eshtar aim carza aj...*
I don't want to see you anymore	Não o/a quero ver mais *now oo/ah kairoo vair mysh*

3.12 Saying goodbye

Can I take you home?	Posso levá-lo/la para casa? *possoo levar loo/la parra carza?*
Can I write/call you?	Posso escrever-lhe/telefonar-lhe? *possoo eshcrevair lya/teleffonar lya?*
Will you write/call me?	Escreve me/telefóna-me? *eshcrev muh/teleffona muh?*
Can I have your address/phone number?	Dá me a sua morada/o seu telefone? *dar muh ah sua morrarda/oo sayoo telefon?*
Thanks for everything	Obrigado por tudo *obrigardoo por toodoo*
It was very nice	Gostei imenso *goshtay immensoo*
Say hello to...	Cumprimentos a... *coomprimentoosh ah...*
All the best	Desejo-te o melhor *dezayjoo tuh oo mellyor*
Good luck	Que tudo corra bem *kuh toodoo corrah baim*
When will you be back?	Quando voltas? *cwarndoo volltash*
I'll be waiting for you	Espero por ti *eshpairoo por tee*
I'd like to see you again	Gostava de voltar a ver-te *goshtarva duh volltar ah vair tuh*
I hope we meet again soon	Espero que a gente volte a se ver brevemente *eshpairoo kuh ah jent vollt ah suh vair brevment*
This is our address. If you're ever in the UK...	Esta é a nossa morada. Se algum dia for à Inglaterra... *eshta eh ah nossa morardah. se algoom deeah for ah eenglaterrah...*
You'd be more than welcome	É sempre bem-vindo *eh semprah baim veendoo*

3

Conversation

31

Eating out

4 Eating out

● **In Portugal** people usually have at least three meals:
Breakfast (*pequeno almoço*) is taken between 7.30 and 10 am. Breakfast is light and consists of *café com leite* (white coffee) and rolls and butter (*pão com manteiga*) or toast (*torradas*).
Lunch (*almoço*) is taken between midday and 2pm. It is usually quite a substantial meal and is never rushed. Offices and shops often close and lunch is taken at home or in a restaurant or café. The meal usually consists of at least two courses and is often preceded by soup. Bread is usually available on the table.
Dinner (*jantar*) is from 8pm onwards and is similar in content to lunch. It is usually a family meal taken at home, except at weekends and public holidays when restaurants are the preferred venue.
Some Portuguese manage to fit in *lanche* (tea) during the afternoon whilst most cannot last until the evening meal without a snack of some sort. Late night supper (*ceia*) is available in some bars and small restaurants around midnight.

4 .1 On arrival

I'd like to book a table for seven o'clock, please	Posso reservar uma mesa para as sete? *possoo resairvar ooma mayza parra ash set?*
I'd like a table for two, please	Uma mesa para duas pessoas, se faz favor *ooma mayza parra dooash pessoash, suh faj favvor*
We've/we haven't booked	(Não) reservámos *(now) resairvarmoosh*
Is the restaurant open yet?	O restaurante já está aberto? *oo reshtowrant jah eshtah abertoo?*
What time does the restaurant open/close?	A que horas abre/fecha o restaurante? *ah kay orash abre/fesha oo reshtowrant?*
Can we wait for a table?	Podemos esperar por uma mesa? *poddaymoosh eshpairar por ooma mayza?*
Will we have to wait long?	Temos de esperar muito tempo? *taymoosh di eshpairar mweentoo tempoo?*
Is this seat taken?	Este lugar está livre? *esht loogar eshtah leevre*
Can we sit here/there?	Podemos sentar aqui/ali? *poodaymoosh sentar akee/alee?*
Can we sit by the window?	Podemos sentar junto à janela? *podaymoosh sentar joontoo ah janella?*
Can we eat outside?	Também podemos comer lá fora? *taubaim poodaymoosh comair la foura?*

Reservou uma mesa?	Do you have a reservation?
Em que nome?	What name, please?
Por aqui, se faz favor	This way, please
Esta mesa está reservada	This table is reserved
Dentro de uns quinze minutos uma mesa fica livre	We'll have a table free in fifteen minutes
Entretanto, importava-se de esperar (no bar)?	Would you like to wait (at the bar)?

Do you have another _____ chair for us?	Pode-nos trazer mais uma cadeira? *pod noosh trazair maiz uma cadairah?*
Do you have a highchair? __	Pode-nos trazer uma cadeira de criança? *pod noosh trazer ooma cadaira de criansa?*
Is there a socket for _____ this bottle-warmer?	Há uma tomada para se ligar este aquecedor de biberão? *hah ooma toomarda parra suh ligar esht akessedor duh beeberow?*
Could you warm up _____ this bottle/jar for me?	Poderia aquecer esta garrafa/este boião? *pooderia akessair eshta garraffa/este boyau?*
Not too hot, please _____	Não muito quente, se faz favor *now mweentoo kent, suh faj favvor*
Is there somewhere I _____ can change the baby's nappy?	Há aqui algum lugar onde eu possa arranjar o bébé? *hah akee algoom loogar ond eu possa arranjar oo behbeh?*
Where are the toilets? _____	Onde são os lavabos? *ond sow oosh lavarboosh?*

4.2 Ordering

Waiter! _____	Senhor empregado!/Garçon! *senyor empregardoo!/garsonn!*
Madam! _____	Minha senhora! *meenya senyora!*
Sir! _____	Senhor! *senyor!*
We'd like something to ____ eat/a drink	Nós gostaríamos de comer/beber alguma coisa *noj goshtariamosh duh commair/bebbair algooma coyza*
Could I have a quick _____ meal?	Poderia comer alguma coisa rapidamente? *pooderia commair algooma coyza rappeedament?*
We don't have much time __	Temos pouco tempo *taymoosh poecoo tempoo*
We'd like to have a _____ drink first	Primeiro queríamos beber qualquer coisa *preemayroo kerriamoosh bebbair qualcair coyza*
Could we see the _____ menu/wine list, please?	Poderia dar nos a ementa/lista de vinhos? *pooderia dar noosh ah ementa/leeshta duh veenyoosh?*
Do you have a menu _____ in English?	Tem uma ementa em inglês? *taim ooma ementa aim inglayj?*
Do you have a dish _____ of the day?	Tem um prato do dia/menu turístico? *taim oom prarto do dia/menu tureeshteeco?*
We haven't made a _____ choice yet	Ainda não escolhemos *eyeenda now eshcolyemoosh*
What do you _____ recommend?	O que é que nos recomenda? *oo kee eh kuh noosh recomenda*
What are the specialities ____ of the region/the house?	Quais são as especialidades da região/da casa? *quysh sow az eshpecialidardesh duh regiau/ duh carza?*
I like strawberries/olives ____	Gosto de morangos/de azeitonas *goshtoo duh morangoosh/de azaytonnash*

I don't like fish/meat...	Não gosto de peixe/de carne *now goshtoo duh paysh/duh carn/duh...*
What's this?	O que é isto? *oo ki eh ishtoo*
Does it have...in it?	Isto leva...? *ishtoo levva?*
What does it look like/ taste like?	Com o que é que se parece?/Tem gosto de quê? *com oo ki eh kuh suh paress?/taim gostoo duh kay?*
Is it a hot or a cold dish?	É um prato frio ou quente? *eh oom prartoo freeoo o kent?*
Is it sweet?	É um prato doce? *eh oom prartoo dose?*
Is it spicy?	É um prato picante/com muitos temperos? *eh oom prartoo picant/com mweentoosh temperoosh?*
Do you have anything else, please?	Tem por acaso outra coisa? *taim por acarzoo ohtra coyza?*
I'm on a salt-free diet	Não posso comer sal *now possoo commair sal*
I can't eat pork	Não posso comer carne de porco *now possoo commair carn duh porcoo*
– sugar	Não posso comer açúcar *now possoo commair assoocar*
– fatty foods	Não posso comer gorduras *now possoo commair gordourash*
– (hot) spices	Não posso comer coisas muito picantes *now possoo commair coyzash mweentoo picantesh*
I'll/we'll have what those people are having	O mesmo que aqueles senhores, se faz favor *oo mejmoo kuh akelesh senyoresh suh faj favvor*
I'd like...	Para mim... *parra me...*
We're not having a starter	Não queremos entrada *now keraymoosh entrarda*
The child will share what we're having	O menino come alguma coisa do nosso prato *oo meneenoo com algooma coyza doo nossoo prartoo*

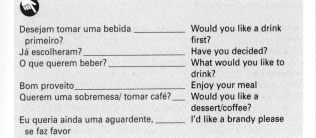

Desejam tomar uma bebida primeiro?	Would you like a drink first?
Já escolheram?	Have you decided?
O que querem beber?	What would you like to drink?
Bom proveito	Enjoy your meal
Querem uma sobremesa/ tomar café?	Would you like a dessert/coffee?
Eu queria ainda uma aguardente, se faz favor	I'd like a brandy please

Could I have some _____ more bread, please?	Traga nos mais pão, se faz favor
	tragga noosh mysh pow, suh faj favvor
– a bottle of water/wine ____	Traga nos uma garrafa de água/de vinho, se faz favor
	tragga nooz ooma garraffa duh agwa/duh veenyoo, suh faj favvor
– another helping of... ____	Traga nos mais uma dose de..., se faz favor
	tragga nooj myz ooma doz duh ..., suh faj favvor
– some salt and pepper ____	Poderia trazer sal e pimenta, se faz favor?
	pooderia trazair sal ee peementa suh faj favvor?
– a napkin _____	Poderia trazer um guardanapo?
	pooderia trazair oom gwardanarpoo?
– a spoon _____	Poderia trazer uma colher?
	pooderia trazair ooma coolyer?
– an ashtray _____	Poderia trazer um cinzeiro?
	pooderia trazair oom seenzayroo?
– some matches_____	Poderia trazer fósforos?
	pooderia trazair foshferoosh?
– some toothpicks_____	Poderia trazer palitos?
	pooderia trazair paleetoosh?
– a glass of water _____	Poderia trazer um copo de água?
	pooderia trazair oom coppoo d'agwa?
– a straw (for the child) ____	Poderia trazer uma palhinha (para o menino)?
	pooderia trazair ooma pallyeenya (parra o meneeno)?
Enjoy your meal! _____	Bom proveito!
	bom proovaytoo
You too! _____	Igualmente!
	eegwalmente
Cheers! _____	À sua saúde!
	ah sooah sowood
The next round's on me ___	A próxima rodada eu pago
	ah prossima roodarda ew pargoo
Could we have a doggy____ bag, please?	Podemos levar o resto para o nosso cão?
	podaymoosh levvar oo reshtoo parra oo nossoo cow?
How much is this dish? ____	Qual é o preço deste prato?
	cuarl eh oo praysoo desht prartoo?

4 .3 The bill

See also 8.2 Settling the bill

Could I have the bill, _____ please?	A conta, se faz favor
	ah conta suh faj favvor
All together _____	Tudo junto
	toodoo joontoo
Everyone pays _____ separately	Cada um paga a sua parte
	carda oom parga ah sooah part
Could we have the menu __ again, please?	Podemos ver a ementa novamente?
	podaymoosh vair ah ementa novvament?
The...is not on the bill ____	O/A...não está na conta
	ah/oo...now eshtah nah conta

It's taking a very_____ long time	Está a demorar muito tempo *eshtah ah demorar mweentoo tempoo*
We've been here an _____ hour already	Já aqui estamos há uma hora *jah akee eshtamoosh ah ooma ora*
This must be a mistake ____	Isto deve ser engano *ishtoo dev sair engarnoo*
This is not what I_____ ordered	Isto não é o que pedi *ishtoo now eh oo que peddee*
I ordered..._____	Pedi um/uma ... *peddee oom/ooma...*
There's a dish missing_____	Falta um prato *falta oom prartoo*
This is broken/not clean ___	Isto está partido/sujo *ishtoo eshtah parteedoo/soojoo*
The food's cold _____	A comida está fria *ah comeeda eshtah freea*
– not fresh _____	A comida não é fresca *ah comeeda now eh freshca*
– too salty/sweet/spicy_____	A comida está salgada/doce/condimentada *ah comeeda eshtah salgarda/doess/condimentarda*
The meat's not done_____	A carne está crua *ah carn eshtah crooa*
– overdone _____	A carne está cozida demais *a carn eshtah coozeeda demysh*
– tough _____	A carne está dura *a carn eh reeja*
– off_____	A carne está estragada *a carn eshtah shtragarda*
Could I have something ___ else instead of this?	Podia trazer me outra coisa em vez disto? *poodia trazair muh ohtra coyza aim vej deeshtoo?*
The bill/this amount is _____ not right	A conta/o total não está certa(o) *ah conta/oo tootal now eshtah sairta(oo)*
We didn't have this_____	Isto não nos foi servido *eeshtoo now nooj foi serveedoo*
There's no paper in the ____ toilet	Não há papel higiénico na casa de banho *now ah papell hijenneecoo nah carza duh bahnyoo*
Do you have a _____ complaints book?	Tem um livro de reclamações? *taim oom leevroo duh reclammasoynsh?*
Will you call the_____ manager, please?	Podia chamar o gerente, se faz favor? *poodia shammar oo jerent, suh faj favvor?*

.5 **P**aying a compliment

That was a wonderful _____ meal	Comemos muito bem *comaymoosh mweentoo baim*
The food was excellent ____	A comida estava excelente *ah comeeda eshtarva eshsellent*
The...in particular was _____ delicious	Principalmente o/a...estava excelente *preencipallment oo/ah...eshtarva eshcellent*

4.6 The menu

aperitivos **appetisers**	legumes **vegetables**	pratos frios **cold dishes**
aves **poultry**	lista dos vinhos **the wine list**	pratos quentes **hot dishes**
bebidas alcoólicas **alcoholic beverages**	marisco **shellfish**	queijo **cheese**
bebidas quentes **hot beverages**	pastelaria/doces **confectionery/**	refrescos **cold drinks**
caça **game**	**desserts**	serviço incluído **service included**
cocktails **cocktails**	salgados **savouries**	sobremesas **sweets**
entradas (quentes/frias) **hot/cold starters**	prato do dia **dish of the day**	sopas **soups**
especialidades (regionais) **(regional) specialities**	prato principal **main course**	
	pratos de carne **meat courses**	

4.7 Alphabetical list of drinks and dishes

açorda/camarões à milanesa com alho **prawns with garlic and breadcrumbs**	ameixas secas **prunes**	batido de... **...milkshake**
açúcar **sugar**	amêndoas **almonds**	bebidas alcoólicas **alcoholic beverages**
agua mineral sem/com gás **sparkling/still mineral water**	ananás **pineapple**	bebidas frescas/ quentes **cool/hot drinks**
	anchova **anchovy**	beringela **aubergine**
aguardente **brandy**	aniz **aniseed**	bica **coffee - expresso**
alcachofra **artichoke**	aperitivos **aperitives**	bife **steak**
alcaparras **capers**	arroz **rice**	bife do lombo **sirloin steak**
alface **lettuce**	assado **roast**	bolachas **biscuits**
alho **garlic**	atum **tuna**	bolo **bun**
alho francês **leek**	avelã **hazelnut**	bolo de chocolate **chocolate bun**
almôndegas **meatballs**	azeitonas **olives**	cabrito **kid**
amêijoas **clams**	bacalhão **cod (dried)**	café (com leite) **coffee (white)**
ameixas **plums**	banana **banana**	caldeirada **stew**
	batatas fritas **chips**	camarões grandes **prawns**
	batatas **potatoes**	camarões **shrimps**

38

canja
broth
caracóis
snails
caranguejo
crab
carioca
coffee - weak,
  without milk
carne
meat
carne de porco
pork
carne picada
ground beef
castanhas
chestnuts
cebola
onion
cebolinha
shallot
cenouras
carrots
cerejas
cherries
cerveja
beer
chá
tea
chantilly
cream
  (whipped)
chouriço
smoked preserved
  sausage
cocktails
cocktails
codorniz
quail
coelho
rabbit
cogumelos
mushrooms
costeleta
cutlet
costeleta de
  porco
pork chop
couve
cabbage
couve-flor
cauliflower
cozido
stew
cravinho
clove

crepes
crepes
croquetes (de carne)
croquettes (meat)
cru
raw
talheres
cutlery
dobrada
tripe
doce
sweet
entradas
starters
ervas
herbs
ervilhas
peas
espargos
asparagus
esparguete
spaghetti
especialidades da
  região
regional
specialities
especiarias
spices
espinafre
spinach
farinha
flour
favas
broad beans
feijão branco/
  encarnado/frade/
  verde
beans: haricot/
  kidney/ green
fiambre
ham
fígado
liver
figo
fig
filé
fillet steak
filete
fillet
filé de vitela
fillet of veal
framboesas
raspberries
frango
chicken

frango no
  churrasco
barbecued chicken
frito
fried
fruta (da época)
fruit (of the season)
frutos do mar
seafood
fumado
smoked
galão
coffee - large white
gaspacho
chilled soup (tomato
  and cucumber)
gelado
ice cream
gelo
ice
grão
chick pea
grelhado
grilled
groselhas
red currents
guisado
stew
imperial
draught beer
iogurte
yogurt
língua-de-vaca
tongue
lagosta
lobster
lagostim
crayfish
laranjas
oranges
legumes
vegetables
leite gordo/meio
  magro/magro
milk - full cream/
  semi skimmed/
  skimmed
lentilhas
lentils
licor
liqueur
limão
lemon
limonada
lemonade

linguado
sole
lista de vinho
wine list
lombo de porco
loin of pork
lombo de vaca
sirloin steak
lulas
squid
maçã
apple
mal passado (bife)
rare (beef)
manteiga
butter
maracujá
passion fruit
margarina
margerine
mariscos
shellfish
marmelada
jam
melão
melon
mexilhões
mussels
milho
sweetcorn
miolos
sweetbreads
morangos
strawberries
morcela
black pudding
mostarda
mustard
mousse de chocolate
chocolate mousse
nata
cream
nozes
nuts
omeleta
omelette
ostras
oysters
ovo quente/cozido/estrelado/escalofad o/ mexido
egg - soft/hard/fried/ poached/scrambled
pão
bread

pãozinho
roll
pêra
pear
pêssego
peach
paio
smoked sausage
panqueque
pancake
pargo
sea bream
passas
raisins
pastel de nata
small custard tart
pastelaria
pastry
pato
duck
peito
breast
peixe
fish
peixe frito (carapau)
small fried fish similar to whitebait
peixe espada
sword-fish
pepino
cucumber
perdiz
partridge
perna de borrego
leg of lamb
perú
turkey
pescada
whiting
pimenta
pepper (condiment)
pimento
green/red pepper
pizza
pizza
polvo
octopus
prato do dia
dish of the day
prato frio/quente
cold/hot course
prato principal
main course
presunto
parma ham

pudim
pudding
pudim flan
creme caramel
queijo
cheese
rabanete
radish
recheado
filled, stuffed
rissol
rissole
robalo
sea bass
rodovalho
turbot
rosbife
roast beef
sal
salt
salada
salad
salada russa
salad with mayonnaise
salgadinhos
savoury snacks
salgado/doce
savoury/sweet
salmão
salmon
salmão fumado
smoked salmon
salmonete
red mullet
salsa
parsley
sandes
sandwich
sardinhas
sardines
seco
dry
serviço (não) incluído
service (not) included
sobremesa
dessert
sopa
soup
sopa de cebola
onion soup
sopa de feijão
bean soup
sumo de fruta
fruit juice

sumo de laranja	torrada	vitela
orange juice	toast	veal
sumo de limão	tosta mista	veado
lemon juice	toasted cheese and	venison
tâmara	ham sandwich	vinagre
fig	toucinho	vinegar
tamboril	bacon	vinho branco
monk fish	truta	white wine
tarte de maçã	trout	vinho rosé
apple tart	truta salmoneja	rosé wine
tomate	salmon trout	vinho tinto
tomato	uvas	red wine
tomilho	grapes	xerez
thyme		sherry

On the road

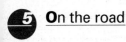

On the road

5.1 **A**sking for directions

Excuse me, could I ask you something? — Desculpe, posso-lhe fazer uma pergunta?
deshcoolp possoo lher fazair ooma pergoonta?

I've lost my way — Perdi-me
perdee muh

Is there a... around here? — Conhece um...perto daqui?
coonyes oom...pairtoo dakee?

Is this the way to...? — É este o caminho para...?
eh esht oo cameenyoo parra...?

Could you tell me how to get to the... (name of place) by car/on foot? — Poderia dizer-me como devo fazer para ir para...a pé/de carro?
pooderia dizair muh como dayvoo fazair parra eer parra...ah peh/duh cahroo?

What's the quickest way to...? — Como é que chego o mais depressa possível a...?
como eh kuh chaygoo oo mysh depressa posseevel ah...?

How many kilometres is it to...? — Quantos quilómetros faltam ainda para chegar a...?
cuarntoosh keelometroosh faltam ayeenda parra sheggar ah...?

Could you point it out on the map? — Poderia indicar-me aqui no mapa?
pooderiah eendiccar muh akee noo mappa?

Não sei, não conheço isto aqui	I don't know, I don't know my way around here
Está enganado	You're going the wrong way
Tem de voltar a...	You have to go back to...
Aí as placas indicam-lhe o caminho a seguir	From there on just follow the signs
Aí deve perguntar de novo	When you get there, ask again

---

em frente	cruzamento	passagem de nível;
straight ahead	intersection	cancelas
à esquerda	estrada	level crossing
left	street	placa indicando o
à direita	semáforo	caminho à...
right	traffic light	sign pointing to...
cortar	placa de trânsito	ponte
turn	`cruzamento com	bridge
seguir	prioridade'	seta
follow	`give way' sign	arrow
atravessar	rio	
cross	river	

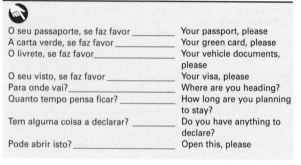

5 .2 Customs

● **Documents**: valid passport, visa. For car and motorbike: valid UK driving licence and registration document, insurance document, green card, UK registration plate. Caravan: must be entered on the green card and be driven with the same registration number. An inventory in either Portuguese, English or French of its contents must be available (this also applies to trailers) to show customs. A warning triangle, headlamp converters and extra headlamp bulbs must be carried. Insurance should also be upgraded.

Import and export specifications:
– Foreign currency: no restrictions
– Alcohol (if aged 17 and above): 10 litres of spirits and 90 litres of wine. Tobacco (if aged 17 and above): 800 cigarettes, 200 cigars or a kilo of tobacco. Restricted to personal consumption only.

O seu passaporte, se faz favor _____	Your passport, please
A carta verde, se faz favor _____	Your green card, please
O livrete, se faz favor_____	Your vehicle documents, please
O seu visto, se faz favor _____	Your visa, please
Para onde vai?_____	Where are you heading?
Quanto tempo pensa ficar? _____	How long are you planning to stay?
Tem alguma coisa a declarar? _____	Do you have anything to declare?
Pode abrir isto?_____	Open this, please

My children are entered ___ on this passport	Os meus filhos estão inscritos neste passaporte *oosh mayoosh feelyoosh eshtau eenshcreetoosh nest passaport*
I'm travelling through _____	Estou de passagem *eshtoe duh passarjaim*
I'm going on holiday to... __	Vou de férias para... *voe duh ferriash parra...*
I'm on a business trip _____	Estou em viagem de negócios *eshtoe aim veearjaim duh neggossioosh*
I don't know how long_____ I'll be staying yet	Ainda não sei quanto tempo fico *ayeenda now say cuarntoo tempoo feecoo*
I'll be staying here for _____ a weekend	Fico aqui um fim-de-semana *feecoo akee oom feem duh semarna*
– for a few days _____	Fico aqui uns dias *feecoo akee unsh deeash*
– for a week_____	Fico aqui uma semana *feecoo akee ooma semarna*
– for two weeks _____	Fico aqui duas semanas *feecoo akee dooash semarnash*
I've got nothing to_____ declare	Não tenho nada a declarar *now tenyoo narda a declarar*
I've got...with me_____	Trago comigo... *trargoo comeegoo...*

44

– ...cartons of cigarettes ___	Trago comigo um pacote de cigarros
	trargoo comeegoo oom pacott de sigaroosh
– ...bottles of... _____	Trago comigo uma garrafa de...
	trargoo comeegoo ooma garrafa duh...
– some souvenirs _____	Trago comigo algumas lembranças
	trargoo comeegoo algoomash lembransash
These are personal _____ effects	Estas são coisas pessoais
	eshtash sow coyzash pessooaish
These are not new _____	Estas coisas não são novas
	eshtash coyzash now sow novash
Here's the receipt _____	Aqui está o recibo
	akee eshtah oo receeboo
This is for private use ____	Isto é para uso pessoal
	eeshtoo eh parra oozoo pessooarl
How much import duty ____ do I have to pay?	Quanto tenho de pagar de direitos?
	cuarntoo tenyoo duh pagar duh diraytoosh?
Can I go now? _____	Posso ir agora?
	possoo eer agoora?

5 .3 Luggage

Porter! _____	Bagageiro!/Carregador!
	bagajayroo!/carreggadoor!
Could you take this_____ luggage to...?	Podia levar esta bagagem para..., se faz favor?
	poodia levvar eshtah bagarjaim parra..., suh faj favvor?
How much do I_____ owe you?	Quanto lhe devo?
	cuarntoo lyer dayvoo?
Where can I find a_____ luggage trolley?	Onde estão os carrinhos para a bagagem?
	onde eshtau oosh careenyoosh parra ah bagarjaim?
Could you store this _____ luggage for me?	Posso colocor esta bagagem no depósito?
	possoo coloocar eshta bagarjaim noo deposittoo?
Where are the luggage ____ lockers?	Onde estão os cofres para bagagem?
	ond eshtau oosh coffresh parra bagarjaim?
I can't get the locker _____ open	Não consigo abrir este cofre
	nau conseegoo abreer esht coffre
How much is it per item ____ per day?	Quanto custa um volume por dia?
	cuarntoo cooshta oom voloom por deah?
This is not my bag/_____ suitcase	Isto não é o meu saco/a minha mala
	eeshtoo now eh oo mayoo sarcoo/ah meenya mala
There's one item/bag/ ____ suitcase missing still	Ainda falta um volume/um saco/uma mala
	ayeenda falta oom voloom/oom sarcoo/ooma mala
My suitcase is damaged ___	A minha mala está danificada
	ah meenya mala eshtah daneefeecarda

aberto	desvio	neve
open	diversion	snow
animais cruzando	devagar	nevoeiro
animals crossing	slow down	fog
auto-estrada (com	espere	obras
portagem)	wait	road works
motorway (with	estacionamento	passagem de nivel
tolls)	parking	(sem guarda)
bermas baixas	estacionamento	level crossing
low hard-shoulder	proibido	(unmanned)
bifurcação	no parking	perigo
road fork	estrada em mau	danger
centro da cidade	estado	portagem
city centre	irregular road	toll
circule pela direita	surface	posto de primeiros
keep right	estrada interrompida	socorros
circule pela esquerda	no through road	First Aid Post
keep left	estrada nacional	saída
cruzamento perigoso	main road	exit
dangerous crossroads	excepto	sentido único
cuidado	except	one-way street
caution	fechado	vedado ao trânsito
curva a...quilómetros	closed	road closed
road bends in...	fim de...	veículos pesados
kilometres	end of...	heavy vehicles
curva perigosa	fim de obras	velocidade máxima
dangerous bend	end of roadworks	maximum speed
dê passegem	gelo	via de acesso
give way	ice on road	access only

5.5 The car

See the diagram on page 49.

● **Particular traffic regulations:**
– maximum speed for cars:
  120km/h on motorways
  90km/h outside built-up areas
  60km/h in built-up areas
– give way: traffic on the main road has priority but at intersections of equal priority traffic from the right has priority

5.6 The petrol station

● **Petrol is** more expensive in Portugal than in many other countries. Portugal has a good network of motorway service stations and filling stations, most of which accept payment by credit card.

How many kilometres to ___   Quantos quilómetros faltam para a
 the next petrol station,   próxima bomba de gasolina?
 please?   *cuarntoosh keelometroosh faltam parra ah*
   prossima bomba de gasooleena?

I would like...litres of..., ____	Quero...litros de...
	kairoo...leetroosh duh...
– super petrol ____	Quero...litros de gasolina super
	kairoo...leeroosh duh gazooleena super
– leaded petrol ____	Quero...litros de gasolina normal
	kairoo...leetroosh duh gazooleena normal
– unleaded petrol ____	Quero...litros de gasolina sem chumbo
	kairoo...leetroosh duh gazooleena saim shoomboo
– diesel ____	Quero...litros de gasóleo
	kairoo...leetroosh duh gazollio
I would like...escudos' ____ worth of..., please	Quero...escudos de..., se faz favor
	kairoo...eshcoodoosh duh..., suh faj favvor
Fill her up, please ____	Encha se faz favor
	ensha suh faj favvor
Could you check...?____	Não se importava de ver...?
	now se importarva duh vair...?
– the oil level ____	Não se importava de ver o nível do óleo?
	now se importarva duh vair oo neevel doo ollio?
– the tyre pressure ____	Não se importava de ver a pressão dos pneus?
	now se importarva duh vair ah pressow doosh penayoosh?
Could you change the ____ oil, please?	Podia mudar o óleo?
	poodia moodar oo ollio?
Could you clean the ____ windows/the windscreen, please?	Podia limpar os vidros/o pára-brisas?
	poodia leempar oosh vidroosh/oo parra-breezash?
Could you give the car____ a wash, please?	Podia dar uma lavagem ao carro?
	poodia dar ooma lavarjaim ow cahroo?

 .7 Breakdown and repairs

I'm having car trouble.____ Could you give me a hand?	Tenho uma avaria. Poderia ajudar-me?
	tenyoo ooma avveriah. pooderia ajoodar-muh?
I've run out of petrol ____	Estou sem gasolina
	eshtoe saim gazoleena
I've locked the keys in ____ the car	Deixei as chaves dentro do carro
	dayshay ash sharvesh dentroo doo cahroo
The car/motorbike/ ____ moped won't start	O carro/a mota/a motorizada não arranca
	oo cahroo/ah motta/ah motoreezarda now aranca
Could you contact____ the rescue service for me, please?	Poderia avisar o pronto socorro da ACP?
	pooderia aveezar oo prontoo socoroo da ey say pay?
Could you call a____ garage for me, please?	Poderia telefonar para uma oficina?
	pooderia telefonar parra ooma offeeseena?

5

The parts of a car
(the diagram shows the numbered parts)

1 battery	bateria	*batteria*
2 rear light	luz da retaguarda	*looj da rettagwarda*
3 rear-view mirror	espelho retrovisor	*eshpelyoo retrooveesor*
reversing light	farol de marcha atrás	*farol duh marcha atraj*
4 aerial	antena	*antenna*
car radio	rádio	*rahdioo*
5 petrol tank	depósito de gasolina	*depozitoo duh gazooleena*
6 sparking plugs	velas	*vellash*
fuel filter/pump	filtro/bomba de gasolina	*feeltroo/bomba duh gazooleena*
7 wing mirror	espelho exterior	*eshpelyoo eshterrior*
8 bumper	pára-choques	*para shocksh*
carburettor	carburador	*carbooradoor*
crankcase	cárter	*cartair*
cylinder	cilindro	*seeleendroo*
ignition	platinados	*platteenardoosh*
warning light	luz de controle	*l ooj duh controal*
dynamo	dínamo	*deenamoo*
accelerator	acelerador	*asselleradoor*
handbrake	travão de mão	*travow duh mau*
valve	válvula	*vallvoola*
9 silencer	silenciador	*seelenciadoor*
10 boot	mala	*marla*
11 headlight	farol da frente	*faroll da frent*
crank shaft	eixo da manivela	*ayshoo da manivela*
12 air filter	filtro do ar	*feeltroo doo ar*
fog lamp	faróis de nevoeiro	*faroysh duh nevooayroo*
13 engine block	motor	*mottor*
camshaft	árvore de cames	*arvora duh camesh*
oil filter/pump	filtro/bomba do óleo	*feeltroo/bomba doo ollio*
dipstick	vareta	*varetta*
pedal	pedal	*pedarl*
14 door	porta	*porta*
15 radiator	radiador	*raddiadoor*
16 brake disc	disco do travão	*deeshcoo doo travow*
spare wheel	roda sobresselente	*rodda sobresallent*
17 indicator	pisca-pisca	*peeshca-peeshca*
18 windscreen wiper	limpa pára-brisas	*leempa parra-breezash*
19 shock absorbers	pára-choques	*parra shocksh*
sunroof	janela do tejadilho	*janella doo taijadeelhoo*
spoiler	spoiler	*spoiler*
starter motor	motor de arranque	*motor di arrank*
20 steering column	caixa de direcção	*caisha duh deeresow*
21 exhaust pipe	tubo de escape	*tooboo duh eshcape*
22 seat belt	cinto de segurança	*seentoo duh seguransa*
fan	ventoinha	*ventooeenya*
23 distributor cables	cabos conductores	*carboosh condootoresh*

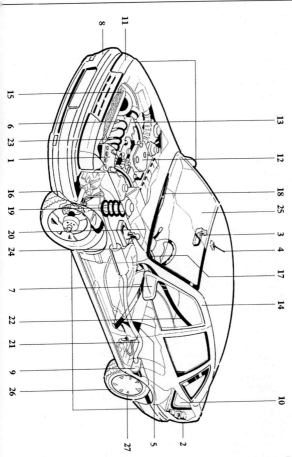

5 On the road

24	gear lever	alavanca das mudanças	alavanca dash moodansash
25	windscreen water pump	pára-brisas bomba de água	parra breezash bomba de agwa
26	wheel	roda	rodda
27	hubcap piston	tampo de roda êmbolo	tampoo duh rodda aimboloo

Could you give me a lift to...?	Posso ir consigo até a...?
	possoo eer conseegoo atay ah...?
– a garage/into town?	Posso ir consigo até a uma oficina/à cidade?
	possoo eer conseegoo atay ooma offiseena/ah sidarda?
– a phone booth?	Posso ir consigo até a uma cabine telefónica?
	Possoo eer conseegoo atay ooma cabeen telefonica?
– an emergency phone?	Posso ir consigo até a um telefone de urgência?
	possoo eer conseegoo atay ah oom telefon duh urgencia?
Can we take my bicycle/moped?	Posso levar também a minha bicicleta/motorizada?
	possoo levar tambaim ah meenya beeceecleta/motoreezarda?
Could you tow me to a garage?	Poderia rebocar-me até a uma garagem?
	pooderia reboocar-muh atay ooma gararjaim?
There's probably something wrong with... (See page 48)	Creio que há algum problema com...
	crayoo kuh ha algoom prooblema com...
Can you fix it?	Poderia consertar isso?
	pooderia consertar eesoo?
Could you fix my tyre?	Poderia consertar-me o pneu?
	pooderia consertar-muh oo punayoo?
Could you change this wheel?	Poderia mudar esta roda?
	pooderia moodar eshta rodda?
Can you fix it so it'll get me to...?	Poderia arranjar isto de maneira que possa seguir até...
	pooderia arranjar eeshtoo duh manayra kuh possoo segear atay...
Which garage can help me?	Que oficina poderá me ajudar?
	kay offiseena poodera muh ajoodar?
When will my car/bicycle be ready?	Quando o meu carro/a minha bicicleta fica pronto/pronta?
	cuarndoo oo mayoo cahroo/ah meenya beeseeclaytah feeca prontoo/pronta?
Can I wait for it here?	Posso esperar aqui?
	possoo eshpairar akee?
How much will it cost?	Quanto é que vai custar?
	cuarntoo eh kuh vy cooshtar?
Could you itemise the bill?	Poderia especificar a factura?
	pooderia eshpeceefeecar ah fatoora?
Can I have a receipt for the insurance?	Pode dar-me um recibo para a companhia de seguros?
	pod dar muh oom receeboo parra ah companyeea duh segooroosh?

Não tenho peças para o seu _____ carro/a sua bicicleta	I don't have parts for your car/bicycle
Tenho de ir buscar as peças em_____ outro lugar	I have to get the parts from somewhere else
Tenho de encomendar as peças_____	I have to order the parts
Isto leva meio-dia_____	That'll take half a day
Isto dura um dia_____	That'll take a day
Isto dura uns dias_____	That'll take a few days
Isto dura uma semana _____	That'll take a week
O seu carro vai para a sucata _____	Your car is a write-off
Já não há nada a fazer _____	It can't be repaired.
O carro/a mota/a motorizada está _____ pronto/pronta às...horas	The car/motor bike/moped/bicycle will be ready at... o'clock.

5.8 The bicycle/moped

See the diagram on page 53.

● **Cycling/riding mopeds** on the roads can be dangerous in Portugal as riders are largely disregarded by motorists, but there are some interesting off-road tracks (unmarked). Rented cycles are few and far between so it is advisable for visitors to bring their own – and a crash helmet.

5.9 Renting a vehicle

I'd like to rent a..._____	Eu gostaria de alugar um... *eyoo goshtaria duh aloogar oom...*
Do I need a (special)_____ licence for that?	Preciso de ter uma carta de condução especial? *preseezoo duh tair ooma carta duh condoosow eshpessial?*
I'd like to rent the...for... ___	Gostaria de alugar o...por... *gostaria duh aloogar oo...por...*
– one day_____	Gostaria de alugar o...por um dia *gostaria duh aloogar oo...por oom deeah*
– two days _____	Gostaria de alugar o...por dois dias *gostaria duh aloogar oo...por doysh deeash*
How much is that per_____ day/week?	Quanto custa por dia/por semana? *cuarntoo cooshta por deeah/por semarna?*
How much is the _____ deposit?	Quanto é o depósito? *cuarntoo eh oo depozeetoo?*
Could I have a receipt _____ for the deposit?	Pode dar-me um recibo do depósito? *pod dar muh oom resseeboo doo depozeetoo?*
How much is the _____ surcharge per kilometre?	Quanto tenho a pagar por cada quilómetro extra? *cuarntoo tenyoo ah paggar por carda keelometroo estra?*
Does that include petrol? __	A gasolina está incluída? *ah gazooleena eshtah eenclooeeda?*
Does that include _____ insurance?	O seguro está incluído? *oo segooroo eshtah eenclooeedoo?*

The parts of a bicycle
(the diagram shows the numbered parts)

1	rear lamp	luz da retaguarda	ooj da retagwarda
2	rear wheel	pneu de trás	penayoo duh traj
3	(luggage) carrier	porta bagagem	porta bagarjaim
4	bicycle fork	caixa de esferas	caysha di eshfairash
5	bell	campainha	campyeenya
	inner tube	câmara de ar	camera di ar
	tyre	pneu	penayoo
6	crank	crenque	crenk
7	gear change	alavanca das velocidades	alavanca dash velocidardesh
	wire	fio	feeoo
	dynamo	dínamo	deenamoo
	bicycle trailer	atrelado para bicicleta	atrellardoo parra beeceeclayta
	frame	quadro	cuardroo
8	dress guard	protector (de vestuário)	prootetor (duh veshtooaryoo)
9	chain	corrente	coorent
	chain guard	caixa de corrente	caisha duh coorent
	chain lock	cadeado de corrente	caddayardoo duh coorent
	milometer	conta quilometros	conta keelometroosh
	child's seat	cadeira para criança	caddayra parra criansa
10	headlamp	farol	faroll
	bulb	lâmpada	lamperdah
11	pedal	pedal	pedarl
12	pump	bomba	bomba
13	reflector	reflector	reflettor
14	break pad	bloco de travão	blocoo duh travow
15	brake cable	cabo de travão	carboo duh travow
16	ring lock	cadeado de algema	cadeeardoo duh aljayma
17	carrier straps	elásticos de porta bagagem	lashteecoosh duh porta bagarjaim
	tachometer	velocimetro	velossimetroo
18	spoke	raio	rayoo
19	mudguard	guarda-lamas	gwarda lamash
20	handlebar	guiador	guiadoor
21	chain wheel	roda de lentes	rodda duh lentesh
	toe clip	gancho	ganshoo
22	crank axle	eixo de pedal	aischoo duh pedarl
	drum brake	jante	jant
23	valve	pipo de válvula	peepoo duh valvoola
24	valve tube	pipo de borracha	peepoo duh borrasha
25	gear cable	cabo de velocidades/ de engrenagem	carboo duh velossidardesh/duh engrenarjaim
26	fork	forqueta	forketta
27	front wheel	roda de frente	rodda duh frent
28	seat	selim	selleem

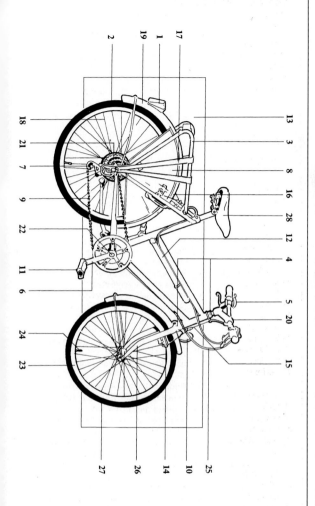

What time can I pick the...up tomorrow?	A que horas posso passar amanhã para vir buscar o/a ...? *ah kay orash possoo passar ahmarnyar parra veer booshcar oo/a ...?*
When does the...have to be back?	Quando tenho de vir entregar o/a ...? *cuarndoo tenyoo duh veer entreggar oo/a ...?*
Where's the petrol tank?	Onde está o depósito? *ond eshtah oo depozeetoo?*
What sort of fuel does it take?	Que tipo de combustível consome? *kuh teepoo duh combushteevel consom?*

5.10 Hitchhiking

Where are you heading?	Para onde vai? *parra ond vy?*
Can I come along?	Posso ir consigo? *possoo eer conseegoo?*
Can my boyfriend/ girlfriend come too?	O meu amigo/a minha amiga também pode ir? *oo mayoo ameegoo/ah meenya ameega tambaim pod eer?*
I'm trying to get to...	Vou para... *voe parra...*
Is that on the way to...?	Fica em caminho à...? *feeca aim cameenyoo ah...?*
Could you drop me off...?	Poderia deixar-me em...? *pooderia dayshar muh aim...?*
– here?	Poderia deixar-me aqui? *pooderia dayshar muh akee?*
– at the...exit?	Poderia deixar-me quando se corta para... *pooderia dayshar muh cuarndoo se corta parra...*
– in the centre?	Poderia deixar-me no centro? *pooderia dayshar muh noo centroo?*
– at the next roundabout?	Poderia deixar-me na próxima rotunda? *pooderia dayshar muh na prosseema rotoonda?*
Could you stop here, please?	Importa-se de parar aqui, se faz favor? *importas duh parar akee suh faj favvor?*
I'd like to get out here	Gostaria de descer aqui *gostaria duh deshsair akee*
Thanks for the lift	Muito obrigado pela boleia *mueentoo obrigahdoo pella boolay*

Public transport

6.1 In general

● In addition to the rather sparse Portuguese rail network, there is a comprehensive long distance coach service with good connections between north Portugal and the Algarve and between most towns and cities. The Portuguese capital, Lisbon, is well-served by its bus network, taxis, river ferries, a small underground railway (undergoing expansion) and special lifts/funiculars for getting up and down the city's seven hills.

Announcements

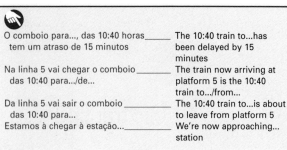

O comboio para..., das 10:40 horas_____ tem um atraso de 15 minutos	The 10:40 train to...has been delayed by 15 minutes
Na linha 5 vai chegar o comboio_____ das 10:40 para.../de...	The train now arriving at platform 5 is the 10:40 train to.../from...
Da linha 5 vai sair o comboio_____ das 10:40 para...	The 10:40 train to...is about to leave from platform 5
Estamos à chegar à estação_____	We're now approaching... station

Where does this train_____ go to?	Para onde vai este comboio? *parra ond vy esht comboyoo?*
Does this boat go to...? ____	Este barco vai para...? *esht barcoo vy parra...?*
Can I take this bus to...? ___	Posso tomar este autocarro para ir para...? *possoo toomar esht owtoocahroo parra eer parra...?*
Does this train _____ stop at...?	Este comboio pára em...? *esht comboyoo para aim...?*
Is this seat taken/free/ _____ reserved?	Este lugar está ocupado/livre/ reservado? *esht loogar eshtar ocoopardoo/ leevre/rezairvardoo?*
I've booked... _____	Reservei... *reservay...*
Could you tell me _____ where I have to get off for... ?	Pode dizer-me onde devo sair para...? *pod deezair muh ond dayvoo sayeer parra...?*
Could you let me_____ know when we get to...?	Podia avisar-me quando chegarmos a...? *poodia aveezar-muh cuarndoo shegarmoosh ah...?*
Could you stop at the_____ next stop, please?	Podia parar na próxima paragem, se faz favor? *poodia parrar nah prosseema pararjaim, suh faj favvor?*

Where are we now? _____	Onde estamos?
	ond eshtarmoosh?
Do I have to get off here? _	Tenho de sair aqui?
	tenyoo duh sayeer akee
Have we already _____ passed...?	Já passámos por...?
	jah passarmoosh por...
How long have I been _____ asleep?	Quanto tempo é que dormi?
	cuarntoo tempoo eh kuh dormee?
How long does... _____ stop here?	Quanto tempo fica...aqui parado?
	cuarntoo tempoo feeca...akee parardoo?
Can I come back on the _____ same ticket?	Também posso voltar com este bilhete?
	tambaim possoo voltar com esht beelyet?
Can I change on this _____ ticket?	Posso mudar com este bilhete?
	possoo moodar com est beelyet?
How long is this ticket _____ valid for?	Quanto tempo é que este bilhete é válido?
	cuarntoo tempoo eh kuh esht beelyet eh vallydoo?

 .2 Questions to passengers

Ticket types

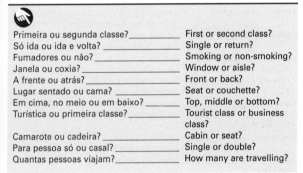

Primeira ou segunda classe?_____	First or second class?
Só ida ou ida e volta? _____	Single or return?
Fumadores ou não? _____	Smoking or non-smoking?
Janela ou coxia? _____	Window or aisle?
A frente ou atrás? _____	Front or back?
Lugar sentado ou cama? _____	Seat or couchette?
Em cima, no meio ou em baixo? _____	Top, middle or bottom?
Turística ou primeira classe?_____	Tourist class or business class?
Camarote ou cadeira? _____	Cabin or seat?
Para pessoa só ou casal? _____	Single or double?
Quantas pessoas viajam?_____	How many are travelling?

Destination

Para onde deseja ir? _____	Where do you wish to go?
Quando deseja partir?_____	When do you wish to leave?
O seu...parte às... _____	Your...leaves at...
Tem de fazer transbordo _____	You have to change trains/ coaches
Tem de sair em... _____	You have to get off at...
Tem de fazer escala por..._____	You have to travel via...
A partida é no dia... _____	The outward journey is on...
O regresso é no dia... _____	The return journey is on...
Tem de estar a bordo das...no máximo	You have to be on board by...

Public transport

O seu bilhete, se faz favor _____	Your ticket, please
A sua marcação, se faz favor _____	Your reservation, please
O seu passaporte, se faz favor _____	Your passport, please
Não está sentado no seu lugar _____	You're in the wrong seat
Está sentado no...errado _____	You're on/in the wrong...
Este lugar está reservado _____	This seat is reserved
Tem de pagar uma taxa _____	You'll have to pay a supplement
Tem um atraso de...minutos _____	There is a delay of... minutes

6 .3 Tickets

Where can I...? _____	Onde é que posso...?
	onde eh kuh possoo...?
– buy a ticket? _____	Onde é que posso comprar um bilhete?
	onde eh kuh possoo comprar oom beelyet?
– make a reservation? _____	Onde é que posso reservar um lugar?
	onde eh kuh possoo rezairvar oom loogar?
– book a flight? _____	Onde é que posso marcar um vôo?
	onde eh kuh possoo marcar oom voe?
Could I have a...to..., please? _____	Queria um...para...?
	kerria oom...para...?
– a single _____	Queria um bilhete só de ida para...?
	kerria oom beelyet soh duh eeda parra...?
– a return _____	Queria um bilhete de ida e volta para...?
	kerria oom beelyet duh eeda e volta parra...?
first class _____	primeira classe
	preemayra clahs
second class _____	segunda classe
	segoonda clahs
tourist class _____	classe turística
	clahs tooreeshteeca
business class _____	classe de negócios
	clahs duh negossyoosh
I'd like to book a seat/couchette/cabin _____	Queria reservar um lugar/uma cama/um camarote
	kerria rezairvar oom loogar/ooma camma/ oom cammarot
I'd like to book a berth in the sleeping car _____	Queria reservar um lugar na carruagem-cama
	kerria rezairvar oom loogar na carrooarjaim camma
top/middle/bottom _____	em cima/no meio/em baixo
	aim seema/noo mayoo/aim byshoo
smoking/no smoking _____	fumadores/não fumadores
	foomadoresh/now foomadoresh
by the window _____	à janela
	ah janella

Public transport

single/double _____	individual/duplo
	indeeveedual/dooploo
at the front/back_____	à frente/atrás
	ah frent/ah traj
There are...of us_____	Somos...pessoas
	somush...pessoash
a car _____	um carro
	oom cahroo
a caravan _____	uma roulotte
	ooma roolot
...bicycles _____	...bicicletas
	...beeseeclaytash
Do you also have...? _____	Também tem...?
	tambaim taim...?
– season tickets? _____	Também tem um bilhete para várias viagens?
	tambaim taim oom beelyet parra varriash veearjainsh?
– weekly tickets? _____	Também tem passe semanal?
	tambaim taim pass semanal?
– monthly tickets? _____	Também tem um passe mensal?
	tambaim taim oom pass mensal?

6 .4 Information

Where...? _____	Onde...?
	ond...?
Where's the information ___ desk?	Onde são as informações?
	ond sow ash eenformasoynsh?
Where can I find a_____ timetable?	Onde está o horário das partidas/chegadas?
	ond eshtah oo orareeoo dash parteedash/sheggardash?
Where's the...desk? _____	Onde é o guiché de...?
	ond eh oo geeshay duh...?
Do you have a city map_____ with the bus/the underground routes on it?	Tem uma planta da cidade com a rede dos autocarros/do metropolitano?
	taim ooma planta dah sidarde com ah reyd dooz outoocahroosh/doo metropooleetarnoo?
Do you have a _____ timetable?	Tem um horário?
	taim oom oraryoo?
I'd like to confirm/_____ cancel/change my booking for/trip to...	Queria confirmar/anular/alterar a marcação/viagem para...
	kerria confeermar/anoolar/alterar ah marcasow/veearjaim parra...
Will I get my money_____ back?	O dinheiro é devolvido?
	oo deenyayroo eh devolveedoo?
I want to go to... _____ How do I get there? (What's the quickest way there?)	Tenho de ir para...Qual é a viagem (mais rápida) para lá?
	tenyoo duh eer parra...cuarl eh ah veearjaim (mysh rappida) parra la?
How much is a _____ single/return ticket to...?	Quanto custa um bilhete de ida/ida e volta para...?
	cuarntoo cooshta oom beelyet duh eeda e volta parra...?

Do I have to pay a _____ supplement?	Tenho de pagar suplemento? *tenyoo duh paggar sooplementoo?*
Can I interrupt my _____ journey with this ticket?	Com este bilhete, posso interromper a viagem? *com esht beelyet possoo eenterompair ah veearjaim?*
How much luggage _____ am I allowed?	Quantos quilos de bagagem posso levar? *cuarntoosh keeloosh duh bagarjaim possoo levar?*
Can I send my luggage ____ in advance?	Posso enviar a minha bagagem com antecedência? *possoo enviar a meenya bagarjaim com antessidencia?*
Does this...travel direct? ___	Este...é directo? *esht...eh deeretoo?*
Do I have to change? _____ Where?	Tenho de fazer transbordo? Onde? *tenyoo duh fazair transhboordoo? ond?*
Will there be any _____ stopovers?	O avião faz escalas? *oo avvyiow faj eshcarlash?*
Does the boat call in at ____ any ports on the way?	O navio pára em alguns portos? *oo naveeoo para aim algoonsh portoosh?*
Does the train/ _____ bus stop at...?	O comboio/camioneta pára em...? *oo comboyoo/camioonayta para aim...?*
Where should I get off? ____	Onde é que devo sair? *ond eh kuh dayvoo syeer?*
Is there a connection _____ to...?	Há ligação para...? *ah leegasow parra...?*
How long do I have to ____ wait?	Quanto tempo tenho de esperar? *cuarntoo tempoo tenyoo duh eshperrar?*
When does...leave?_____	Quando é que parte...? *cuarndoo eh kuh part...?*
What time does the _____ first/next/last...leave?	A que horas é o primeiro/próximo/último...? *ah kay orash eh oo preemayroo/prosseemoo/oolteemoo...?*
How long does...take? ____	Quanto tempo leva...? *cuarntoo tempoo levva?*
What time does...arrive ____ in...?	A que horas chega...a...? *ah kay orash shayga...ah...?*
Where does the...to... _____ leave from?	Donde parte o...para...? *dond part oo...parra...?*
Is this...to...? _____	É este...para...? *eh esht...parra...?*

6.5 Aeroplanes

● **At a Portuguese airport** (*aeroporto*), you will find the following signs:

chegadas	voos domésticos	alfândega
arrivals	domestic flights	customs
partidas	internacional	
departures	international	

.6 Trains

● **The Portuguese rail network** is still being developed and
upgraded, but there are fast services between the main cities of Lisbon
and Oporto

.7 Taxis

● **Metered taxis** are available in all cities and large towns and are
usually black and green. In the smaller towns, it is usual to agree a
fixed price in advance as well as to check that the meter starts the
journey at zero. A supplement is normally payable for luggage, a
journey at night and on sundays or public holidays, but Portuguese
taxis are generally cheaper than taxis in the rest of Europe.

livre	ocupado	praça de táxis
for hire	booked	taxi rank

Taxi! _____ — Táxi!
tarksy!

Could you get me a taxi, ___ — Podia chamar um táxi?
please? — *poodia shammar oom tarksy?*

Where can I find a taxi ___ — Onde é que posso apanhar um táxi,
around here? — aqui perto?
ond eh kuh possoo apanyar oom tarksy akee pairtoo?

Could you take me to..., ___ — Podia levar-me para..., se faz favor?
please? — *poodia levah muh parra..., suh faj favvor?*

– this address _____ — Podia levar-me para esta morada, se faz
favor?
poodia levah muh parra eshta morrarda, suh faj favvor?

– the...hotel _____ — Podia levar-me para o hotel..., se faz
favor?
poodia levah muh parra oo ohtel..., suh faj favvor?

– the town/city centre _____ — Podia levar-me para o centro, se faz
favor?
poodia levah muh parra oo sentroo, suh faj favvor?

– the station _____ — Podia levar-me para a estação, se faz
favor?
poodia levah muh parra ah eshtasow, suh faj favvor?

– the airport _____ — Podia levar-me ao aeroporto se faz
favor?
poodia levah muh ow ayroopoortoo, suh faj favvor?

How much is the _____ — Qual é o preço da viagem para...?
trip to...? — *cuarl eh oo praysoo dah veearjaim parra...?*

How far is it to...? _____ — Qual é a distância até...?
cuarl eh ah deeshtarnsia atay...?

Could you turn on the _____ — Pode ligar o taxímetro, se faz favor?
meter, please? — *pod leegar oo tazkseemetroo, suh faj favvor?*

Public transport

61

I'm in a hurry _____	Estou com pressa
	eshtoe com pressa
Could you speed up/ _____ slow down a little?	Podia guiar mais depressa/mais devagar?
	poodia guiar mysh depressa/mysh deevagar?
Could you take a _____ different route?	Podia ir por outro caminho?
	poodia eer por ohtroo cameenyoo?
I'd like to get out here, _____ please	Deixe-me ficar aqui, se faz favor
	daysh muh feecar akee, suh faj favvor
You have to go...here _____	Tem de ir aqui...
	taim duh eer akee...
You have to go straight ____ on here	Tem de ir aqui em frente
	taim duh eer akee aim frent
You have to turn left_____ here	Tem de ir aqui à esquerda
	taim duh eer akee ah eshkairda
You have to turn right _____ here	Tem de ir aqui à direita
	taim duh eer akee ah dirayta
This is it _____	É aqui
	eh akee
Could you wait a minute___ for me, please?	Podia esperar um momento?
	poodia eshperar oom moomentoo?

Overnight accommodation

Overnight accommodation

7 .1 General

● *Hoteis (hotels):* these are classified according to the standard of comfort offered and range from five star de luxe to simple one star, priced accordingly. The same applies to aparthotels and motels.
Pousadas: these are extremely well-appointed state-owned hotels located either in historic buildings or areas of particular natural beauty.
Estalagens: these are usually restored buildings similar to *pousadas* but privately owned and offering a good level of accommodation.
Habitacões de Turismo: these offer short-stay accommodation in large and beautiful private residences similar to stately homes. The owners are often present and the level of comfort varies.
Pensões, residências, albergarias: these are usually less expensive and offer a lesser degree of comfort than the other forms of accommodation. They are also classified and sometimes visitors to Portugal may fare better in a highly classified *residência* or *albergaria* than in a low rated hotel.
Camping: camping away from the one hundred or so designated camp sites is not usually allowed.
Albergos da juventude: there are very few youth hostels in Portugal. There is no upper age limit. Advance booking at peak times is advisable.

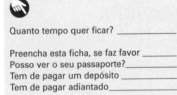

Quanto tempo quer ficar? _____	How long do you want to stay?
Preencha esta ficha, se faz favor _____	Fill out this form, please
Posso ver o seu passaporte?_____	Could I see your passport?
Tem de pagar um depósito _____	I'll need a deposit
Tem de pagar adiantado_____	You'll have to pay in advance

My name is... I've made ___ a reservation (over the phone/by mail/by fax)	Chamo-me... Reservei um lugar/um quarto (pelo telefone/por escrito/por fax) *shammoo muh...rezervay om loogar/oom cuartoo (pelloo telefon/poor eshcreetoo/poor fax)*
How much is it per _____ night/week/month?	Qual é o preço por noite/por semana/por mês? *cuarl eh oo praysoo por noyt/por semarna/por mayge?*
We'll be staying at _____ least...nights/weeks	Ficamos pelo menos...noites/semanas *feecarmoosh pello menoosh... noytsh/semarnash*
We don't know yet _____	Ainda não sabemos precisamente *ayeenda now sabbaymoosh preseezament*
Do you allow pets _____ (cats/dogs)?	É permitido trazer animais domésticos (cães/gatos)? *eh pairmeeteedo trazair aneemysh doomeshteecoosh (caynsh/gartoosh)?*

What time does the _____ gate/door open/close?	A que horas abrem/fecham a cancela/a porta? *ah kay orash abraim/feysham ah cancella/ah porta?*
Could you get me _____ a taxi, please?	Poderia mandar vir um táxi? *pooderia mandar veer oom tacksy?*
Is there any mail _____ for me?	Há correio para mim? *ah coorayoo parra meem?*

7.2 Camping

See the diagram on page 69.

See the diagram on page 69.

Pode escolher o seu lugar _____	You can pick your own site
Nós lhe indicamos um lugar _____	You'll be allocated a site
Este é o número do seu lugar _____	This is your site number
Importa-se de colar isto no seu carro?___	Stick this on your car, please
Não perca este cartão _____	Please don't lose this card

Where's the manager? _____	Onde está o responsável? *ond eshtah oo reshponsarvel?*
Are we allowed to _____ camp here?	Podemos acampar aqui? *poodaymoosh acampar akee?*
There are...of us and we ___ have...tents	Somos...pessoas e temos...tendas *somoosh...pessoash e taymoosh...tendash*
Can we pick our _____ own site?	Nós próprios podemos escolher um lugar? *nosh propreeoosh poodaymoosh eshcoolyair oom loogar?*
Do you have a quiet _____ spot for us?	Poderia dar-nos um lugar tranquilo? *pooderia dar noosh oom loogar trankeeloo?*
Do you have any other ___ pitches available?	Não tem um outro lugar livre? *now taim oom ohtroo loogar leevre?*
It's too windy/sunny/ _____ shady here.	Aqui há muito vento/sol/muita sombra *akee ah mweentoo ventoo/sol/mweenta sombra*
It's very crowded here _____	Há muita gente *ah mweenta jent*
The ground's too _____ hard/uneven	O chão aqui é muito duro/desigual *oo shau akee eh mueentoo dooroo/deseeguarl*
Do you have a level _____ spot for the camper/ caravan/folding caravan?	Poderia arranjar um lugar plano para o reboque/a rulote/o trailer? *pooderia arranjar oom loogar plarnoo parra oo rabok/a roolot/oo trailer?*
Could we have adjoining ___ pitches?	Podemos ficar juntos? *poodaymoosh feecar joontoosh?*
Can we park the car _____ next to the tent?	Pode-se estacionar o carro perto da tenda? *pod suh eshtasionar oo cahroo pairtoo da tenda?*

How much is it per _____ person/tent/caravan/car?	Quanto custa por pessoa/tenda/rulote/carro? *cuarntoo cooshta por pessoah/tenda/roolot/cahroo?*
Are there any...? _____	Há...? *ah...?*
– hot showers? _____	Há duches com água quente? *ah dooshesh com agwa kent?*
– washing machines? _____	Há máquinas de lavar? *ah markeenash duh lavar?*
Is there a...on the site? _____	Há neste parque um...? *ah nesht park oom...?*
Is there a children's _____ play area on the site?	Há neste parque um jardim infantil? *ah nesht park oom jardeem eenfanteel?*
Are there covered _____ cooking facilities on the site?	Há neste parque um lugar coberto para cozinhar? *ah nesht park oom loogar coobairtoo parra coozeenyar?*
Can I rent a safe here? _____	Posso alugar um cofre? *possoo alloogar oom cofre?*
Are we allowed to _____ barbecue here?	Pode-se fazer churrasco aqui? *pod suh fazair choorashcoo akee?*
Are there any power _____ points?	Há tomadas de corrente eléctrica? *ha toomardash duh corrent eeletreeca?*
Is there drinking water? ____	Há água potável? *ah agwa pootarvel?*
When's the rubbish _____ collected?	Quando recolhem o lixo? *cuarndoo recolyaim oo leeshoo?*
Do you sell gas bottles ____ (butane gas/ propane gas)?	Vende garrafas de gás (butagás/gás propano)? *vende garrafash duh gaj (bootagaj/gaj prooparnoo)?*

.3 Hotel/B&B/apartment/holiday house

Do you have a _____ single/double room available?	Tem um quarto simples/de casal livre? *taim oom cuartoo seemplesh/duh cazal leevre?*
How much is it per _____ person/per room?	Qual é o preço por pessoa/por quarto? *cuarl eh oo praysoo por pessoa/por cuartoo?*
Does that include _____ breakfast/lunch/dinner?	Já está incluido pequeno almoço/almoço/jantar? *jah eshtah eenclooeedoo peekaynoo almohsoo/almohsoo/jantar?*
Could we have two _____ adjoining rooms?	Pode arranjar dois quartos juntos? *pod arranjar doysh cuartoosh joontoosh?*
I'd like a room with/ _____ without toilet/bath/ shower	Queria um quarto com/sem casa de banho/banheira/duche individual *kerria oom cuartoo com/saim carza duh barnyoo/banyayra/doosh eendeeveedual*
I'd like a room _____ (not) facing the street	Queria um cuarto (não) para o lado da rua *kerria oom cuartoo (now) parra oo lardoo da rooah*

I'd like a room with/without a view of the sea	Queria um cuarto com/sem vista para o mar *kerria oom cuartoo com/saim veeshta parra oo mar*
Is there...in the hotel?	O hotel tem... *o ohtel taim...*
Is there a lift in the hotel?	O hotel tem elevador? *oo ohtel taim eelevadoor?*
Do you have room service?	O hotel tem serviço de quarto? *oo ohtel taim serveesoo duh cuartoo?*
Could I see the room?	Posso ver o quarto? *possoo vair oo cuartoo?*
I'll take this room	Fico com este quarto *feecoo com esht cuartoo*
We don't like this one	Este não nos agrada *esht now noos agrarda*
Do you have a larger/less expensive room?	Tem um quarto maior/mais barato? *taim oom cuartoo myor/mysh barartoo?*
Could you put in a cot?	Poderia pôr aqui uma cama de criança? *pooderia poor akee ooma carma duh creeansa?*
What time's breakfast?	A que horas servem o pequeno almoço? *ah kay orash servaim oo peekaynoo almohsoo?*
Where's the dining room?	Onde é a sala de jantar? *ond eh a sarla duh jantar?*
Can I have breakfast in my room?	Posso tomar o pequeno almoço no quarto? *possoo toomar oo peekaynoo almohsoo noo cuartoo?*
Where's the emergency exit/fire escape?	Onde fica a saída de emergência/escada de incêndio? *ond feeca ah sayeeda duh emergensia/eshcarda duh eensendeeoo?*
Where can I park my car (safely)?	Onde há um lugar (seguro) para estacionar o meu carro? *ond ah oom loogar (segooroo) parra eshtassionar oo mayoo karoo?*
The key to room..., please	A chave do quarto..., se faz favor *a sharv doo cuartoo..., suh faj favvor*
Could I put this in your safe, please?	Posso pôr isto no seu cofre? *possoo poor eeshtoo noo sayoo cofre?*

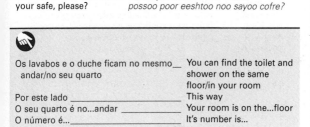

Os lavabos e o duche ficam no mesmo andar/no seu quarto	You can find the toilet and shower on the same floor/in your room
Por este lado	This way
O seu quarto é no...andar	Your room is on the...floor
O número é...	It's number is...

Camping equipment
(the diagram shows the numbered parts)

	luggage space	parte resguardo para a bagagem	part reshgwardoo parra ah bagarjaim
	can opener	abre-latas	abre lartash
	butane gas bottle	garrafa de gás	garrafa duh gaj
		saco para bicicleta	sarcoo parra beeceeclayta
1	pannier	fogão de campismo	foogow duh campeejmoo
2	primus stove	oleado	olliardoo
3	groundsheet	martelo	martelloo
	mallet	rede	reyd
	hammock	jerrican	gerrican
4	jerry can	fogueira	foogayra
	campfire	cadeira dobrável	cadayra doobrarvel
5	folding chair	geladeira	geladayra
6	insulated picnic box	almofadas de geladeira	almoofardash duh geladayra
	ice pack	bússola	boosolla
	compass	camisa	cameeza
	wick	saca-rolhas	saca rolyash
	corkscrew	cama inflável	carma eenflarvel
7	airbed	pipo	peepoo
8	airbed plug	bomba de ar	bomba di ar
	pump	toldo	toldoo
9	awning	tapete	tappett
10	karimat	panela	panella
11	pan	asa de panela	arza duh panella
12	pan handle	feixo	fayshoo
	zip	mochila	mosheela
13	backpack	espia	eshpeea
14	guy rope	saco de dormir	sarcoo duh dormeer
	sleeping bag	lanterna	lantairna
15	storm lantern	cama de campismo	carma duh campeejmoo
	camp bed	mesa	mayza
	table	tenda	tenda
16	tent	cavilha	caveelya
17	tent peg	estaca da tenda	eshtarca da tenda
18	tent pole	termos	termoosh
	vacuum flask	cantil	canteel
19	water bottle	mola da roupa	molla da roepa
	clothes peg	arame	ararm
	clothes line	pára-vento	parra ventoo
	windbreak	lanterna de bolso	lantairna duh bolsoo
20	torch	canivete	cannivet
	pocket knife		

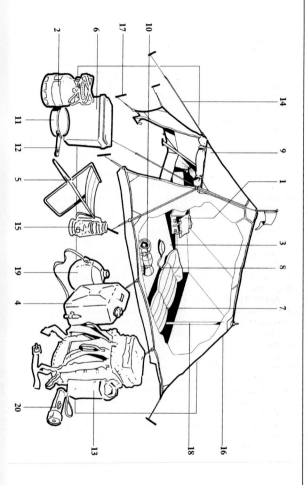

Could you wake me _____ at...tomorrow?	Poderia acordar-me amanhã às ...? *pooderia acordar muh armanyar ash ...?*
Could you find a _____ babysitter for me?	Poderia ajudar-me a arranjar uma pessoa para tomar conta do bébé? *pooderiah ajoodar muh ah arranjar ooma pessoa parra toomar conta do baybay?*
Can I have an extra_____ blanket?	Arranja-me um outro cobertor, se faz favor? *arranj muh oom ohtroo coobertor, suh faj favvor?*
What days do the _____ cleaners come in?	Em que dia fazem a limpeza? *aim kuh deeah farzaim uh leempayza?*
When are the sheets/ _____ towels/tea towels changed?	Quando é que são mudados os lençóis/as toalhas/os panos de cozinha? *cuarndoo eh kuh sow moodardash oosh lensoysh/ash tooalyash/oosh parnoosh duh coozeenya?*

7.4 Complaints

We can't sleep because _____ of the noise	Não conseguimos dormir devido ao barulho *now consegeemoosh doormeer deveedoo ow baroolyoo*
Could you turn the _____ radio down, please?	Pode pôr o rádio um pouco mais baixo? *pod poor oo rardeeoo oom pohcoo maiz abyshoo?*
We're out of toilet paper ___	Acabou-se o papel higiénico *acarboe suh oo papell eegenneecoo*
There isn't any.../there's_____ not enough...	Não há.../não há...suficiente *now ah.../now ah...soofeecient*
The bed linen's dirty_____	A roupa de cama está suja *a roepa duh carma eshtah sooja*
The room hasn't been _____ cleaned	O quarto não foi limpo *oo cuartoo now foy leempoo*
The kitchen is not clean_____	A cozinha não foi limpa *a coozeenya now foy leempa*
The kitchen utensils are_____ dirty	Os utensílios de cozinha estão sujos *ooz ootenseelyoosh duh cozeenya eshtow soojoosh*
The heater's not_____ working	O aquecimento não funciona *oo akessimentoo now fooncyonna*
There's no (hot) _____ water/electricity	Não há água (quente)/electricidade *now ah agwa (kent)/eeletreecidard*
...is broken_____	...está estragado *...eshtah eshtragardoo*
Could you have that_____ seen to?	Poderia mandar arranjar? *pooderia mandar arranjar?*
Could I have another _____ room/site?	Poderia arranjar um outro quarto/lugar para a tenda? *pooderia arranjar oom ohtroo cuartoo/loogar parra a tenda*
The bed creaks terribly ___	A cama faz muito barulho *a cahma faj mweentoo baroolyoo*
The bed sags _____	A cama baixa muito no meio *a cahma bysha mweentoo no mayoo*

There are bugs/insects_____	Há muitos bichos/insectos
	ah mweentoosh beeshoosh/eensectoosh
This place is full_____	Isto está cheio de mosquitos
of mosquitos	*eeshtoo eshtah shayoo duh moshkeetsch*
– cockroaches_____	Isto está cheio de baratas
	eeshtoo eshtah shayoo duh barattash

 **.5 D**eparture

See also 8.2 Settling the bill

I'm leaving tomorrow._____	Saio amanhã. Posso pagar agora?
Could I settle my bill,	*sayoo armanyar. possoo paggar agoara?*
please?	
What time should we_____	A que horas temos de deixar...?
vacate?	*a kay orash taymoosh duh dayshar...?*
Could I have my_____	Pode devolver-me o depósito/o meu
deposit/passport back?	passaporte?
	pod devolvair muh oo deposeetoo/oo
	mayoo passaport?
We're in a terrible hurry ___	Estamos com muita pressa
	eshtarmoosh com mueenta pressa
Could you forward _____	Poderia enviar-me o correio para esta
my mail to this address?	morada?
	pooderia enviar muh oo corrayoo parra
	eshta morarda?
Could we leave our_____	Podemos deixar as malas aqui até
luggage here until we	irmos embora?
leave?	*poodaymoosh dayshar ash malash akee*
	atay eermoosh emboora?
Thank you very much ____	Muito obrigado pela hospitalidade
for your hospitality	*mweentoo obrigahdoo pella*
	oshpeetalidade

7

Overnight accommodation

Money matters

Money matters

● **In general,** banks in Portugal are open to the public between
8.30am and 3pm, Monday to Friday, but closing times may vary and
smaller branches may close for lunch. The sign *câmbio* indicates that
foreign currency may be exchanged and proof of identity, usually in the
form of a passport, will be required by Portuguese banks. Hotels will
usually change money but at less favourable rates. Portugal has a large
network of cash machines outside the banks and by using a UK-issued
PIN number, money changing is very quick and simple.

8.1 **B**anks

Where can I find a _____ bank/an exchange office around here?	Onde é que há um banco/uma casa de câmbio por aqui? *ond eh kuh ah oom bancoo/ooma carza duh cambyoo poor akee?*
Where can I cash this_____ traveller's cheque/giro cheque?	Onde posso trocar este traveller cheque/cheque do correio? *ond possoo troocar esht traveller shek/shek doo coorayoo?*
Can I cash this...here? ____	Posso trocar este...aqui? *possoo troocar esht...akee?*
Can I withdraw money_____ on my credit card here?	Posso levantar dinheiro aqui com um cartão de crédito? *possoo levantar deenyayroo akee com oom cartow duh credeetoo?*
What's the minimum/_____ maximum amount?	Qual é o mínimo/máximo? *cuarl eh oo meeneemoo/masseemoo?*
Can I take out less_____ than that?	Também posso levantar menos? *tambaim possoo levantar menoosh?*
I've had some money_____ transferred here. Has it arrived yet?	Pedi uma transferência telegráfica. Já chegou? *pedee ooma transhferensia telegraffeeca. Jah shegoe?*
These are the details _____ of my bank in the UK	Estes são os dados do meu banco na Grã Bretanha *eshtesh sow oosh dardoosh doo mayoo bancoo nah grar bretarnya*
This is my bank/giro_____ number	Este é o número da minha conta bancária/no correio *esht eh oo noomeroo da meenya conta bancaria/noo coorayoo*
I'd like to change _____ some money	Eu gostarià de trocar dinheiro *eyoo goshtaria duh troocar deenyayroo*
– pounds into... _____	Eu gostarià de trocar libras esterlinas por... *eyoo goshtaria duh troocar leebrash eshterleenash por...*
– dollars into... _____	Eu gostarià de trocar dólares americanos por... *eyoo goshtaria duh troocar dollaresh amereecarnoosh por...*
What's the exchange _____ rate?	Qual é o câmbio? *cuarl eh oo carmbio?*

Could you give me _____ some small change?	Podia dar-me também dinheiro trocado, por favor?	
	poodia dar muh tambaim deenyayroo troocardoo por favvor?	
This is not right _____	Isto está errado	
	eeshtoo eshtah eerardoo	

Tem de assinar aqui_____	You have to sign here
Tem de preencher isto _____	You have to fill this out
Mostra-me o seu passaporte? _____	Could I see your passport?
Mostra-me o seu bilhete _____ de identidade?	Could I see some identification?
Mostra-me o seu cartão dos correios?___	Could I see your girobank card?
Mostra-me o seu cartão do banco?_____	Could I see your bank card?

8 .2 Settling the bill

Could you put it on_____ my bill?	Pode enviar para a minha conta?	
	pod enviar parra ah meenya conta?	
Does this amount _____ include service?	O serviço está incluído?	
	oo sairveesoo schtah eenclooeedoo?	
Can I pay by...?_____	Posso pagar com...?	
	possoo paggar com...?	
Can I pay by credit card?___	Posso pagar com um cartão de crédito?	
	possoo paggar com oom cartow duh craydeetoo?	
Can I pay by traveller's ____ cheque?	Posso pagar com um traveller cheque?	
	possoo pagar com oom traveller shek?	
Can I pay with foreign _____ currency?	Posso pagar com moeda estrangeira?	
	possoo paggar com mooayda eshtranjayra?	
You've given me too _____ much/you haven't given me enough change	Deu-me dinheiro a mais/menos	
	dayoo muh deenyayroo ah mysh/menoosh	
Would you like to check ___ the bill again?	Quer verificar a conta novamente?	
	care vereefeecar ah conta novvamentjee?	
Could I have a receipt? ____	Pode dar-me um recibo/talão da caixa?	
	pod dar muh oom resseeboo/talow da caisha?	
I don't have enough _____ money on me	Não tenho comigo dinheiro suficiente	
	now tenyoo comeegoo deenyayroo soofeecient	
This is for you _____	Faça favor, isto é para si	
	fassa favvor eeshtoo eh parra see	

Não se aceita cartões de crédito/_____ traveller cheques/moeda estrangeira	Credit cards/traveller's cheques/foreign currency are not accepted

Post and telephone

Post and telephone

9 .1 **P**ost

● **Most post offices** *(correios)* are open from 9am to 5pm from Monday to Friday and until 1pm on Saturdays. Some smaller post offices close for lunch between 12.30pm and 2.30pm. Stamps *(selos)* are also sold in tobacconists' shops *(tabacarias)* displaying the sign *CTT selos*. Portuguese postboxes are red.

vales postais	telegramas	selos
money orders	telegrams	stamps
encomendas		
parcels		

Where's...?	Onde é...?
	ond eh...?
Where's the post office?	Onde é o correio mais perto?
	ond eh oo coorayoo mysh pairtoo?
Where's the main post office?	Onde é a agência principal do correio?
	ond eh a ajencia preenceepal doo coorayoo?
Where is the postbox?	Há aqui perto uma caixa de correio?
	ah akee pairtoo ooma caisha duh coorayoo?
Which counter is for...?	Qual é o guiché para...?
	cuarl eh oo geeshay para...?
– sending a fax?	Qual é o guiché para enviar um fax?
	cuarl eh oo geeshay parra enviar oom fax?
– changing money?	Qual é o guiché para trocar dinheiro?
	cuarl eh oo geeshay parra troocar deenyayroo?
– giro cheques?	Qual é o guiché para os cheques `giro'?
	cuarl eh oo geeshay parra oosh sheksh jeero?
– money orders?	Qual é o guiché para vale telegráfico?
	cuarl eh oo geeshay parra val telegrarfeecoo?
Poste restante	Posta-restante
	poshta reshtant
Is there any mail for me?	Há correio para mim?
	ah c@rayoo parra meem.
My name's...	O meu nome é...
	Oo mayoo nom eh...

Stamps

What's the postage for a...to...?	Quanto custa um/uma...para...?
	cuarntoo cooshta oom/ooma...parra...?
Are there enough stamps on it?	Este valor de selos chega?
	esht valor duh seloosh shayga?
I'd like...stamps of...escudos	Queria...selos de...escudos
	kerria...seloosh duh...eshcoodoosh
I'd like to send this...	Queria enviar isto...
	kerria enviar eeshtoo...

– by express _____	Queria enviar isto por expresso
	kerria enviar eeshtoo poor eshpraysoo
– by air mail _____	Queria enviar isto por correio aéreo
	kerria enviar eeshtoo por coorayoo airayoo
– by registered mail _____	Queria enviar isto registado
	kerria enviar eeshtoo regeeshtardoo

Telegram/fax

I'd like to send a _____ telegram to...	Queria enviar um telegrama para...
	kerria enviar oom telegrarma parra...
How much is it per _____ word?	Quanto custa cada palavra?
	cuarntoo cooshta cadda palarvra?
This is the text I want_____ to send	Este é o texto que quero enviar
	esht eh oo teshtoo kuh kerria enviar
Shall I fill out the form_____ myself?	Posso preencher eu próprio o impresso?
	possoo pre-enshair eyoo propreeoo oo eempraysoo?
Can I make photocopies/___ send a fax here?	Posso fazer fotocópias/enviar um fax aqui?
	possoo fazair fotoocopiash/enviar oom fax akee?
How much is it_____ per page?	Quanto custa por página?
	cuarntoo cooshta por parjeena?

9.2 Telephone

See also 1.8 Telephone alphabet

● **As in most** countries, telephone calls made from hotels are
expensive. Most public telephones offer a direct international service,
but as only low value coins can be used, a considerable quantity must
be on hand. Cardphones are available and phone cards *(cartão
credifone)* can be purchased from post offices. Portugal is well-served
by the global mobile telephone network (GSM) and so it is well worth
taking one along. Unlike in the UK, it is perfectly in order to ring
someone after 9.30pm.

Is there a phone box _____ around here?	Há aqui perto uma cabine telefónica?
	ah akee pairtoo ooma cabeen telefoneeca?
Could I use your _____ phone, please?	Posso utilizar o seu telefone, se faz favor?
	possoo ooteeleezar oo sayoo telefon, suh faj favvor?
Do you have a _____ (city/region)...phone directory?	Tem uma lista telefónica de.../da zona de...?
	taim ooma leeshta telefoneeca duh.../duh zona duh...?
Where can I get a _____ phone card?	Onde é que posso comprar um cartão credifone?
	ond eh kuh possoo comprar oom cartow credifon?
Could you tell me...?_____	Podia dizer-me...?
	poodia deezair muh...?

– the number for _____ international directory enquiries?	Podia dizer-me o número das informações internacionais? *poodia deezair muh oo noomeroo daz eenformasoynsh eenternacionysh?*
– the number of room...? __	Podia dizer-me o número do quarto...? *poodia deezair muh oo noomeroo doo cuartoo...?*
– the international _____ access code?	Podia dizer-me o indicativo de acesso? *poodia deezair muh oo eendeecateevoo duh assesoo?*
– the country code for...?___	Podia dizer-me o indicativo de...? *poodia deezair muh oo eendeecateevoo duh...?*
– the trunk code for...? _____	Podia dizer-me o indicativo da zona de...? *poodia deezair muh oo eendeecateevoo da zona duh...?*
– the number of...? _____	Podia dizer-me o número do assinante...? *poodia deezair muh oo noomeroo doo asseenant...?*
Could you check if this _____ number's correct?	Podia verificar se este número está correcto? *poodia vereefeecar see esht noomeroo eshtah cooretoo?*
Can I dial international_____ direct?	Posso telefonar directamente para o estrangeiro? *possoo telefonar deeretament parra oo eshtranjayroo?*
Do I have to go through ___ the switchboard?	Tenho de pedir a chamada à telefonista? *tenyoo de pedeer a shamarda ah telefoneeshta?*
Do I have to dial '0' first? __	Tenho de ligar primeiro o zero? *tenyoo de leegar preemayroo oo zayroo?*
Do I have to book _____ my call?	Tenho de pedir a chamada? *tenyoo de pedeer ah shamarda?*
Could you dial this _____ number for me?	Podia ligar para este número? *poodia leegar parra esht noomeroo?*
Could you put me _____ through to.../extension...?	Podia ligar-me com.../a extensão...? *poodia leegar muh com.../ah eshtensow...?*
I'd like to place a _____ reverse-charge call to...	Queria fazer uma chamada paga para... *kerria fazair ooma shamarda parga parra...?*
What's the charge per _____ minute?	Quanto custa por minuto? *cuarntoo cooshta poor meenootoo?*
Have there been any _____ calls for me?	Alguém telefonou para mim? *algaim telefonoe parra meem?*

The conversation

Hello, this is..._____	Está? Daqui fala... *eshtah? Dakee fala...*
Who is this, please? _____	Quem fala, se faz favor? *caim fala, suh faj favvor?*
Is this...? _____	Estou a falar com...? *eshtoe a falar com...?*

I'm sorry, I've dialled _____ the wrong number	Desculpe, enganei-me no número
	deshcoolp, enganay muh noo noomeroo
I didn't understand what ___ you said	Não compreendi o que disse
	now compreyendee oo kuh deece
I'd like to speak to... _____	Gostava de falar com...
	goshtarva duh falar com...
Is there anybody _____ who speaks English?	Há alguém que fale inglês?
	ah algaim kuh fala inglaij?
Extension..., please_____	Extensão..., se faz favor
	eshtensow..., seh faj favvor
Could you ask him/her_____ to call me back?	Podia pedir-lhe para me telefonar?
	poodia peddeer lya parra muh telefonar?
My name's... _____ My number's...	O meu nome é... O meu número é...
	oo mayoo nom eh... oo meu noomeroo eh...
Could you tell him/her _____ I called?	Podia dizer-lhe que eu telefonei?
	poodia deezair lya kuh eyoo telefonay
I'll call back tomorrow _____	Volto a telefonar-lhe amanhã
	voltoo ah telefonar lya armanyar

Telefone para o senhor/a senhora _____	There's a phone call for you
Ligue primeiro o zero _____	You have to dial '0' first
Aguarde um momento _____	One moment, please
Ninguém atende _____	There's no answer
O número está impedido _____	The line's engaged
Podia esperar?_____	Could you hold?
Vou ligar _____	Putting you through
O número não está correcto _____	You've got the wrong number
Ele/ela não está neste momento _____	He's/she's not here right now
Ele/ela volta... _____	He'll/she'll be back...
Está ligado ao receptor automático _____	This is the answering machine of...

Shopping

10

● **Opening times:** Monday to Friday from 9am to 1pm and 3 to 7pm. On Saturdays shops close at 1pm, but there is a growing trend towards staying open in the afternoons. Shopping centres *(centro comercial)* are also open on Sundays and public holidays from 9am to 1pm, with longer opening hours towards Christmas. Some small shops stay open all day on Sundays. Supermarkets *(supermercado)* stay open until at least 10pm. Chemists' *(farmácia)* opening hours are the same as those of shops and the names of late-night duty chemists are displayed in the shop window and in the newspapers.

loja de antiguidades antique shop	drogaria hardware shop	mercearia grocery store
armazém department store	electrodomésticos electrical appliances	óptica optician's
artigos de desporto sports shop	farmácia pharmacy/ dispensing chemist	padaria bakery
artigos dietéticos health-food		pastelaria cake shop
artigos de segunda mão second-hand goods	feira fleamarket	peixaria fishmonger
artigos fotográficos camera shop	florista florist's	perfumaria perfumery
auto-serviço self-service	frutaria greengrocer's	quiosque kiosk
cabeleireiro hairdresser	geladaria ice-cream parlour	reparação de bicicletas bicycle repairs
casa de bicicletas bicycle shop	joalharia jewellery shop	retrosaria drapers
casa de brinquedos toy shop	lavandaria launderette/ laundry	salão de beleza beauty parlour
casa de móveis furniture shop	leitaria dairy products shop	sapataria shoe shop
casa de vinhos off-licence	limpeza a seco dry-cleaner's	sapateiro cobbler
centro comercial shopping centre	livraria bookshop	supermercado supermarket
decoração de interiores interior design	loja shop	tabacaria tobacconist's
delicatessen delicatessen	loja de modas dress shop	talho butcher's
discoteca/artigos musicais record shop	loja de recordações souvenir shop	
	mercado market	

10.1 Shopping conversations

Where can I get...?	Em que loja posso arranjar...?
	aim kay lohja possoo arranjar...?
When does this shop open?	Quando é que esta loja está aberta?
	cuarndoo eh kuh eshta lohja eshtah aberta?
Could you tell me where the...department is?	Poderia dizer-me onde fica a secção de...?
	pooderia deezer muh ond feeca ah secksow duh...?
Could you help me? I'm looking for...	Pode atender-me? Procuro...?
	pod atendair muh? Procooroo...?
Do you sell English/ American newspapers?	Tem jornais ingleses?
	taim jornysh inglayzesh?

Já está a ser atendido? — **Are you being served?**

No. I'd like...	Não. Queria...
	now. Kerria...
I'm just looking, if that's all right	Só estou a ver, obrigado
	soh eshtoe a vair, obrigahdoo

Mais alguma coisa? — **Anything else?**

Yes, I'd also like...	Sim, dê-me também...
	seem, day muh tambaim...
No, thank you. That's all	Não, muito obrigado. É tudo
	now mueento obrigahdoo. Eh toodoo
Could you show me..., please?	Pode deixar-me ver..., se faz favor?
	pod dayshar muh vair..., suh faj favvor?
I'd prefer...	Eu preferia...
	eyoo prefferia...
This is not what I'm looking for	Isto não é o que eu procuro
	eeshtoo now eh oo kuh eyoo procooroo
Thank you. I'll keep looking	Muito obrigado. Vou dar mais uma volta
	mweentoo obrigahdoo. voe dar maiz ooma volta
Do you have something...?	Não tem nada mais...?
	now taim narda mysh...?
– cheaper?	Não tem nada mais barato?
	now taim narda mysh barartoo?
– smaller?	Não tem nada mais pequeno?
	now taim narda mysh peekaynoo?
– larger?	Não tem nada maior?
	now taim narda myor?
I'll take this one/these	Levo este(s)/esta(s)
	levoo esht (esh)/eshta (sh)

Shopping

Does it come with instructions?	O modo de emprego está lá dentro?
	oo modoo di empraygoo eshtah la dentroo?
It's too expensive	Acho demasiado caro
	achoo demaziardoo caroo
I'll give you...	Ofereço-lhe...
	oferessoo lya...
Could you keep this for me? I'll come back for it later	Importa-se de me guardar isto? Volto já a buscar
	eemporta suh duh muh gwardar eeshtoo? Voltoo jah booshcar
Have you got a bag?	Tem um saco?
	taim oom sarcoo?
Could you giftwrap it, please?	Pode embrulhar como prenda, se faz favor?
	pod embrulyar comoo prenda, suh faj favvor?

Lamento, mas não temos	I'm sorry, we don't have that
Lamento, já não temos mais	I'm sorry, we're sold out
Lamento, só vamos receber isso dentro de...	I'm sorry, that won't be in until...
Pode pagar na caixa	You can pay at the cash desk
Não aceitamos cartões de crédito	We don't accept credit cards
Não aceitamos traveller cheques	We don't accept traveller's cheques
Não aceitamos moedas estrangeiras	We don't accept foreign currency

10 .2 Food

I'd like a hundred grams of...	Eu queria cem gramas de...
	eyoo kerria saim grarmash duh ...
– five hundred grams/ half a kilo of...	Eu queria meio quilo de...
	eyoo kerria mayoo keeloo duh...
– a kilo of...	Eu queria um quilo de...
	eyoo kerria oom keeloo duh...
Could you...?	Importa-se de...?
	eemporta suh duh...?
Could you slice it/ dice it, please?	Importa-se de cortar em fatias/bocados, se faz favor?
	eemporta suh duh cortar aim fateeash/boocardoosh, suh faj favvor?
Could you grate it, please?	Importa-se de o ralar, se faz favor?
	eemporta suh duh oo rallar, suh faj favvor?
Can I order it?	Posso encomendar?
	possoo aincoomendar?
I'll pick it up tomorrow/ at...	Venho buscar amanhã/às...horas
	venyoo booshcar armanyar/ush...orash

Can you eat/drink this? ____ Pode-se comer/beber?
pod se coomair/bebbair

What's in it? _____ De que é feito?
duh kee eh faytoo?

🔟 .3 Clothing and shoes

I saw something in the ____ Vi uma coisa na montra. Posso lhe
window. Shall I point it mostrar?
out? *vee ooma coyza na montra. possoo lya*
mooshtrar?

I'd like something to_____ Queria uma coisa para condizer com
go with this isto
kerria ooma coyza parra condeezair com
eeshtoo

Do you have shoes_____ Tem sapatos nesta mesma cor?
in this same colour? *taim sapartoosh neshta mejma cor?*

I'm a size...in the UK_____ Na Grã Bretanha o meu número é...
na grar bretarnya oo mayoo noomeroo
eh...

Can I try this on? _____ Posso experimentar?
possoo eshprimentar?

Where's the fitting room? _ Onde fica o gabinete de prova?
ond feeca oo gabeenet duh provva?

It doesn't fit_____ Não me serve
now muh sairve

This is the right size _____ Esta medida é boa
eshta medeeda eh boa

It doesn't suit me_____ Não me fica bem
now muh feeca baim

Do you have this/ _____ Tem também isto em...
these in...? *taim tambaim eeshtoo aim...*

I find the heel too high/low Acho o salto demasiado alto/baixo
ashoo oo saltoo demaziardoo altoo/byshoo

Is this genuine leather? ____ Isto é couro verdadeiro?
eeshtoo eh cooroo verdadayroo?

I'm looking for a..._____ Procuro um...para um bébé/uma criança
for a...-year-old de...anos
baby/child *procooroo oom...parra oom baybay/ooma*
criansa duh...arnoosh

I'd prefer a...of... _____ Eu preferia um...de...
eyoo prefferia oom...duh...

– silk _____ Eu preferia um...de seda
eyoo prefferia oom...duh sayda

– cotton _____ Eu preferia um...de algodão
eyoo prefferia oom...duh algoodow

– wool_____ Eu preferia um...de lã
eyoo prefferia oom... duh lang

– linen_____ Eu preferia um...de linho
eyoo prefferia oom...duh leenyoo

What temperature_____ A que temperatura é que posso lavar?
can I wash it at? *a kay temperatoora eh kuh possoo lavar?*

Will it shrink in the _____ Encolhe ao lavar?
wash? *aincollye ow lavar?*

Não passar a ferro	Pendurar molhado	Lavar à mão
Do not iron	Drip dry	Hand wash
Não centrifugar	Limpar a seco	Lavar à máquina
Do not spin dry	Dry clean	Machine wash

At the cobbler's

Could you mend _____ these shoes?	Pode arranjar-me estes sapatos? *pod arranjar muh eshtash sapartoosh?*
Could you put new _____ soles/heels on these?	Poderia pôr aqui solas novas/saltos novos? *pooderia poor akee solash novash/saltoosh novoosh?*
When will they be _____ ready?	Quando estão prontos? *cuarndoo eshtow prontoosh?*
I'd like... _____	Eu queria... *eyoo kerria...*
– a tin of shoe polish _____	Eu queria uma caixa de pomada *eyoo kerria ooma caisha duh poomarda*
– a pair of shoelaces_____	Eu queria um par de atacadores *eyoo kerria oom par duh attackadooresh*

10 .4 Photographs and video

I'd like a film for this_____ camera, please	Eu queria um rolo para esta máquina, se faz favor *eyoo kerria oom rolloo parra eshta markina, suh faj favvor*
– a cartridge _____	Eu queria uma cassette *eyoo kerria ooma cassett*
– a slide film _____	Eu queria um rolo de diapositivos *eyoo kerria oom rolloo duh diaposeeteevoosh*
– a film cartridge _____	Eu queria um cassette para filmar *eyoo kerria oom cassett parra feelmar*
– a videotape _____	Eu queria um cassette de vídeo *eyoo kerria oom cassett duh veedyoo*
– a colour/black and _____ white film	Eu queria um rolo a cores/a preto e branco *eyoo kerria oom rolloo ah cooresh/ah praytoo e brancoo*
– a super eight film_____	Eu queria um filme super de 8mm *eyoo kerria oom feelm soopair duh 8mm*
– a 12/24/36 exposures_____ film	Eu queria um rolo de 12/24/36 fotografias *eyoo kerria oom rolloo duh 12/24/36 fotografeeash*
– a film of...ASA_____	Eu queria um rolo de ISO... *eyoo kerria oom rolloo duh ee ess oo...*
– a daylight film_____	Eu queria um rolo para luz natural *eyoo kerria oom rollo parra looj naturarl*
– a film for artificial light___	Eu queria um rolo para luz artificial *eyoo kerria oom rolloo parra looj artifeeciarl*

Shopping

10

Problems

Could you load the _____
film for me?
Importa-se de colocar o rolo na máquina?
eemporta suh duh coloocar oo rolloo na markina?

Could you take the film _____
out for me?
Importa-se de tirar o rolo da máquina?
eemporta suh duh teerar oo rolloo da markina?

Should I replace _____
the batteries?
Tenho de substituir as pilhas?
tenyoo duh soobshteetweer ash peelyash?

Could you have a look _____
at my camera? It's not working
Importa-se de ver a minha máquina/câmara? Não trabalha
eemporta suh duh vair a meenya markina/camera? Now trabalya

The...is broken _____
O...está estragado
oo...eshtah eshtragardoo

The film's jammed _____
O rolo está preso
oo rolloo eshtah prayzoo

The film's broken _____
O rolo está partido
oo rolloo eshtah parteedoo

The flash isn't working _____
O flash não funciona
oo flash now foonsyona

Processing and prints

I'd like to have this film _____
developed/printed
Eu queria mandar revelar/ reproduzir este rolo
eyoo kerria mandar revelar/ reprodoozeer esht rolloo

I'd like...prints from _____
each negative
Eu queria...cópias de cada negativo
eyoo kerria...copeeash duh cadda negateevoo

I'd like glossy/mat prints _____
Eu queria cópias brilhantes/mates
eyoo kerria copeeash breelyantesh/matsh

I'd like 6x9 prints _____
Eu queria cópias seis por nove
eyoo kerria copeeash saysh poor nov

I'd like to order _____
these photos
Eu queria encomendar estas fotos
eyoo kerria aincoomendar eshtash fotoosh

I'd like to have this _____
photo enlarged
Eu queria mandar ampliar esta foto
eyoo kerria mandar ampliar eshta fotoo

How much is _____
processing?
Quanto custa a revelação?
cuarntoo cooshta a revellasow?

How much is printing? _____
Quanto custa a reprodução?
cuarntoo cooshta a reprodoosow?

How much is it _____
to re-order?
Quanto custa mandar fazer mais cópias?
cuarntoo cooshta mandar fazair mysh copeeash?

How much is an _____
enlargement?
Quanto custa uma ampliação?
cuarntoo cooshta ooma ampleeasow?

When will they _____
be ready?
Quando estão prontas?
cuarndoo eshtow prontash?

Do I have to make an _____ appointment?	Tenho de marcar hora? *tenyoo duh marcar ora?*
Can I come in straight _____ away?	Pode atender-me já? *pod atendair muh jah?*
How long will I have_____ to wait?	Quanto tempo tenho de esperar? *quarntoo tempoo tenyoo duh eshpairar?*
I'd like a hairwash/ _____ haircut	Eu queria lavar/cortar o meu cabelo *eyoo kerria lavar/cortar oo mayoo cabayloo*
I'd like a shampoo for _____ oily/dry hair	Eu queria um champô para cabelo gorduroso/seco *eyoo kerria oom shampoh parra cabayloo gordooroso/saycoo*
– an anti-dandruff _____ shampoo	Eu queria um champô contra a caspa *eyoo kerria oom shampoh contra a cashpa*
– a shampoo for_____ permed/coloured hair	Eu queria um champô para cabelo com permanente/pintado *eyoo kerria oom shampoh parra cabayloo com permanent/peentardoo*
– a colour rinse shampoo __	Eu queria um champô com cor *eyoo kerria oom shampoh com cor*
– a shampoo with conditioner	Eu queria um champô com condicionador *eyoo kerria oom shampoh com condicionardoor*
– highlights _____	Eu queria madeixas *eyoo kerria madayshash*
Do you have a colour_____ chart, please?	Tem um catálogo com as cores? *taim oom cataloggoo com ash coresh?*
I want to keep it the _____ same colour	Eu queria manter a mesma cor *eyoo kerria mantair a mejma cor*
I'd like my hair _____ darker/lighter	Eu queria o cabelo mais escuro/claro *eyoo kerria oo cabayloo maiz eshcooroo/claroo*
I'd like/I don't want _____ hairspray	Quero (não quero) laca no meu cabelo *cairoo (now cairoo) larca noo mayoo cabayloo*
– gel_____	Quero (não quero) gel *cairoo (now cairoo) jel*
– mousse _____	Quero (não quero) mousse *cairoo (now cairoo) mousse*
I'd like a short fringe _____	Queria a franja curta *kerria a franja coorta*
Not too short at the back __	Atrás não queria demasiado curto *atraj now kerria demaziardoo coortoo*
Not too long here _____	Aqui não quero muito comprido *akee now cairoo mweentoo coompreedoo*
I'd like (just a few) curls___	Quero (não muitos) caracóis *cairoo (now mueentoosh) carracoysh*
It needs a little/_____ a lot taken off	Corte um pouco/bastante *cort oom poecoo/bashtant*
I want a completely _____ different style	Queria um modelo totalmente diferente *kerria oom moodeloo tootalment deeferent*
I'd like it as..._____	Queria o meu cabelo como... *kerria oo mayoo cabayloo comoo...*

– that lady's _____	Queria o meu cabelo como o daquela senhora
	kerria oo may cabayloo comoo oo dakella senyora
– in this photo _____	Queria o meu cabelo como o desta foto
	kerria oo mayoo cabayloo comoo oo desta fotoo
Could you put the _____ drier up/down a bit?	Podia pôr o secador mais forte/fraco?
	poodia poor oo secadoor maish fort/frarcoo?
I'd like a facial _____	Queria uma máscara para o rosto
	kerria ooma mashcara parra oo roshtoo
– a manicure _____	Queria que me fizesse uma manicure
	kerria kuh me feezess ooma manicure
– a massage _____	Queria uma massagem
	kerria ooma massarjaim
Could you trim _____ my fringe?	Podia aparar-me a franja?
	poodia aparar muh a franja?
– my beard? _____	Podia aparar-me a barba?
	poodia aparar muh a barba?
– my moustache? _____	Podia aparar-me o bigode?
	poodia aparar muh oo beegod?
I'd like a shave, please _____	A barba, se faz favor
	a barba, se faj favvor
I'd like a wet shave _____	Queria a barba feita com navalha
	kerria a barba fayta com navaly

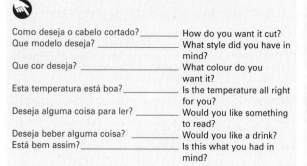

Como deseja o cabelo cortado? _____	How do you want it cut?
Que modelo deseja? _____	What style did you have in mind?
Que cor deseja? _____	What colour do you want it?
Esta temperatura está boa? _____	Is the temperature all right for you?
Deseja alguma coisa para ler? _____	Would you like something to read?
Deseja beber alguma coisa? _____	Would you like a drink?
Está bem assim? _____	Is this what you had in mind?

At the Tourist Information Centre

11 At the Tourist Information Centre

11 .1 Places of interest

Where's the Tourist Information Centre?	Onde é o posto de turismo? *ond eh oo poshtoo duh tooreeshmoo?*
Do you have a city map?	Tem uma planta da cidade? *taim ooma planta dah sidarde?*
Where is the museum?	Onde é o museu? *ond eh oo moozayoo?*
Where can I find a church?	Onde há uma igreja? *ond ah ooma eegrayja?*
Could you give me some information about...?	Podia dar-me alguma informação sobre...? *poodia dar muh algooma eenformasow sobre...?*
How much do we have to pay you?	Quanto é que temos de lhe pagar? *cuarntoo eh kuh taymoosh duh lya pagar?*
What are the main places of interest?	Quais são as atrações mais importantes? *quysh sow ash atrasoynsh maiz eemportantesh?*
Could you point them out on the map?	Podia indicá-las no mapa? *poodia eendeecar lash noo marpa?*
What do you recommend?	O que é que nos aconselha? *oo kuh eh kuh nooz aconselya?*
We'll be here for a few hours	Ficamos aqui umas horas *feecarmoos akee oomash orash*
– a day	Ficamos aqui um dia *feecarmoos akee oom deah*
– a week	Ficamos aqui uma semana *feecarmoos akee ooma semarna*
We're interested in...	Estamos interessados em... *eshtarmoosh eenteressardoosh aim...*
Is there a scenic walk around the city?	Podemos fazer um passeio turístico pela cidade? *poodaymoosh fazair oom passayoo tooreeshteecoo pella sidarde?*
How long does it take?	Quanto tempo demora? *cuarntoo tempoo demoora?*
Where does it start/end?	Onde começa/acaba? *ond comessa/acarba?*
Are there any boat cruises here?	Há aqui barcos de excursão? *ah akee barcoosh duh eshcoorsow?*
Where can we board?	Onde é que podemos embarcar? *ond eh kuh poodaymoosh embarcar?*
Are there any bus tours?	Há excursões de autocarro? *ah eshcoorsoynsh duh outoocahroo?*
Where do we get on?	Onde é que podemos entrar? *ond eh kuh poodaymoosh entrar?*
Is there a guide who speaks English?	Há um guia que fale inglês? *ah oom gueeah kuh fal eenglayj?*

What trips can we take around the area?	Que passeios podemos dar nos arredores?
	kay passayoosh poodaymoosh dar nooz arredooresh?
Are there any excursions?	Há excursões?
	ah eshcoorsoynsh?
Where do they go to?	Para onde vão as excursões?
	parra ond vow az eshcoorsoynsh?
We'd like to go to...	Nós queremos ir a...
	nosh kerraymooz eer ah...
How long is the excursion?	Quanto tempo demora a excursão?
	cuarntoo tempoo demoora ah eshcoorsow?
How long do we stay in...?	Quanto tempo ficamos em...?
	cuarntoo tempoo feecarmoosh aim...?
Are there any guided tours?	Há visitas guiadas?
	ah veezeetash gueeardash?
How much free time will we have there?	Quanto tempo temos só para nós?
	cuarntoo tempoo taymoosh soh parra noj?
We want to go hiking	Queriamos fazer uma caminhada
	kerriamoosh fazair ooma cameenyarda
Can we hire a guide?	Podemos contratar um guia?
	poodaymoosh contratar oom gueeah?
Can I book mountain huts?	Posso reservar abrigos?
	possoo resairvar abreegoosh?
What time does... open/close?	A que horas abre/fecha...?
	ah kay orash abre/faysha...?
What days is...open/ closed?	Em que dias está aberto/fechado...?
	aim kuh deeash eshtah abairtoo/fechardoo...?
What's the admission price?	Quanto custa a entrada?
	cuarntoo cooshta ah entrarda?
Is there a group discount?	Há desconto para grupos?
	ah deshcontoo parra groopoosh?
Is there a child discount?	Há desconto para crianças?
	ah deshcontoo parra creeansash?
Is there a discount for pensioners?	Há desconto para reformados?
	ah deshcontoo parra reformardoosh?
Can I take (flash) photos/can I film here?	Posso aqui fotografar (com flash)/filmar?
	possoo akee fotografar (com flash)/feelmar?
Do you have any postcards of...?	Vende postais com...?
	vend pooshtysh com...?
Do you have an English...?	Tem um/uma...em inglês?
	taim oom/ooma...aim eenglayj?
– catalogue?	Tem um catálogo em inglês?
	taim oom catalogoo aim eenglayj?
– programme?	Tem um programa em inglês?
	taim oom proogramma aim eenglayj?
– brochure?	Tem um folheto em inglês?
	taim oom foolyetoo aim eenglayj?

11

11 .2 Going out

● **There are far fewer cinemas in Portugal** than in the UK.
Usherettes will normally expect a small tip. Most films shown are in
English with Portuguese subtitles, which is very convenient.
Sometimes the name given to the film in Portuguese is completely
different from its original. Details of theatre and cinema programmes
are to be found in the national newspapers, especially in the Friday
editions. Showings are generally much later than in the UK and theatre
performances are often subject to considerable delay.

Do you have this _____ week's/month's entertainment guide?	Tem o jornal de espectáculos desta semana/deste mês? *taim oo jornarl di eshpetarcooloosh deshta semarna/deshta mayge?*
What's on tonight? _____	O que é que há para fazer esta noite? *oo kee eh kuh ah parra fazzair eshta noyt?*
We want to go to... _____	Queríamos ir a... *kerriamoosh eer ah...*
Which films are showing? _	Que filmes estão a passar? *kuh feelmesh eshtow ah passar?*
What sort of film is it? _____	Que género de filme é? *kuh jenroo duh feelm eh?*
It's suitable for all ages _____	É para todas as idades *eh parra toedaz az eedardesh*
It's only for people above _ 12/16 years	É só para pessoas acima dos 12/16 anos *eh sooh parra pessowash aseema dooz 12/16 arnoosh*
It's the original version _____	É a versão original *eh ah versow ooreegeenarl*
It's subtitled_____	É com legendas *eh com lejendash*
It's dubbed_____	É dobrado *eh doobrardoo*
Is it a continuous _____ showing?	São sessões contínuas? *sow sessoynsh conteenooash?*
What's on at...? _____	Qual é o programa do...? *quarl eh oo proograrma doo...?*
– the theatre? _____	Qual é o programa do teatro? *quarl eh oo proograrma doo teeartroo?*
– the concert hall?_____	Qual é o programa de concertos? *quarl eh oo proograrma duh consairtoosh?*
– the opera? _____	Qual é o programa da ópera? *quarl eh oo proograrma dah ohpairah?*
Where can I find a good _ disco around here?	Onde é que há uma boa discoteca aqui? *ond eh kuh ha ooma boa deeshcooteca akee?*
Does one have to be a_____ member?	É necessário ser membro? *eh necessaryoo sair membroo?*
Where can I find a good _ nightclub around here?	Onde é que há um bom clube nocturno aqui? *ond eh kuh ah oom bom cloob notoornoo akee?*
Is it evening wear only? _	É obrigatório traje de cerimónia? *eh obreegatoryoo trarj duh cerimonnia?*

92

Should I/we dress up? _____	É aconselhável traje a preceito? *eh aconselyarvel trarj ah presaytoo?*
What time does the _____ show start?	A que horas começa o show? *ah kay orash coomessa oo show?*
When's the next soccer ____ match?	Quando é o próximo jogo de futebol? *cuarndoo eh oo prosseemoo jogoo duh* *footebol?*
Who's playing?_____	Quem é que vai jogar? *caim eh kuh vy joogar?*
I'd like an escort for _____ tonight. Could you arrange that for me?	Queria ter um/uma acompanhante para hoje a noite. Pode tratar-me disto? *kerria tair oom/ooma acompanyant parra* *oarje a noyt. pod tratar muh deeshtoo?*

11 .3 Booking tickets

We'd like to book... _____	Queríamos reservar... *kerriamoosh rezairvar...*
– seats in the stalls _____	Queríamos reservar...lugares na plateia *kerriamoosh rezairvar...loogaresh na* *plataya*
– seats on the balcony _____	Queríamos reservar...lugares no balcão *kerriamoosh rezairvar...loogaresh noo* *balcow*
– a table at the front_____	Queríamos reservar uma mesa à frente *kerriamoosh rezairvar ooma mayza ah* *frent*
– seats in the centre _____	Queríamos reservar...lugares a meio *kerriamoosh rezairvar...loogaresh ah* *mayoo*
– seats at the back_____	Queríamos reservar...lugares atrás *kerriamoosh rezairvar...loogaresh atraj*
Could I book...seats for _____ the...o'clock performance?	Posso reservar...lugares para a sessão das...? *possoo resairvar...loogaresh parra a* *sessow dash...?*
Are there any tickets left ___ for tonight?	Ainda há bilhetes para esta noite? *ayeenda ah beelyetsch parra eshta noyt?*
How much is a ticket? _____	Quanto custa um bilhete? *cuarntoo cooshta oom beelyet?*
When can I pick the _____ tickets up?	Quando é que posso levantar os bilhetes? *cuarndoo eh kuh possoo levantaroosh* *beelyetsch?*
I've got a reservation _____	Reservei *resairvay*
My name's... _____	O meu nome é... *oo mayoo nom eh...*

At the Tourist Information Centre

11

Para que sessão é que deseja reservar?	Which performance do you want to book for?
Onde é que deseja se sentar?	Where would you like to sit?
Está esgotado	Everything's sold out
Só há lugares de pé	We've only got standing spaces left
Só há lugares no balcão	We've only got balcony seats left
Só há lugares na geral	We've only got seats left in the gallery
Só há lugares na plateia	We've only got stalls seats left
Só há lugares à frente	We've only got seats left at the front
Só há lugares atrás	We've only got seats left at the back
Quantos lugares deseja?	How many seats would you like?
Tem de levantar os bilhetes antes das...horas	You'll have to pick up the tickets before...o'clock
Posso ver os seus bilhetes?	Tickets, please
Este é o seu lugar	This is your seat
Estâo em lugares errados	You're in the wrong seats

Sports

12 Sports

12.1 Sporting questions

Where can we... _____ around here?	Onde é que podemos...aqui? *ond eh kuh poodaymooz...akee?*
Is there a... _____ nearby?	Há um...perto daqui? *ah oom...pairtoo dackee?*
Can I hire a...here? _____	Posso alugar um/uma...aqui? *possoo aloogar oom/ooma...akee?*
Can I take...lessons? _____	Posso ter lições de...? *possoo tair leesoynsh duh...?*
How much is it per _____ hour/per day/a turn?	Quanto custa por hora/dia/vez? *cuarntoo cooshta por ora/deeah/vaij?*
Do I need a permit? _____	É preciso uma licença? *eh preseezoo ooma leesensa?*
Where can I get _____ the permit?	Onde é que posso tirar a licença? *ond eh kuh possoo teerar a leesensa?*

12.2 By the waterfront

Is it a long way (by foot) ___ to the sea?	É.muito longe (a pé) daqui ao mar? *eh mueentoo lonj (ah peh) dakee ow mar?*
Is there...nearby? _____	Há um/uma...perto daqui? *ah akee oom/ooma...pairtoo dackee?*
– an outdoor/indoor/ _____ public swimming pool nearby?	Há uma piscina perto daqui? *ah ooma peeshseena pairtoo dackee?*
– a sandy beach nearby? ___	Há aqui uma praia de areia perto? *ah akee ooma prya di araya pairtoo?*
– a nudist beach nearby? __	Há uma praia de naturistas perto daqui? *ah ooma prya duh natooreeshtash pairtoo dackee?*
– a quay nearby? _____	Há um cais perto daqui? *ah oom kysh pairtoo dackee?*
Are there any rocks _____ here?	Há rochas aqui? *ah roshash akee?*
When's high/low tide? _____	Quando é a maré cheia/a maré vazia? *cuarndoo eh a maray shaya/a maray vazeeah?*
What's the water _____ temperature?	Qual é a temperatura da água? *cuarl eh a temperatoora da agwar?*
Is it (very) deep here? _____	Aqui é (muito) fundo? *akee eh mweentoo foondoo?*
Can I reach the ground _____ here?	Aqui tenho pé? *akee tenyoo peh?*
Is it safe to swim here? ___	É seguro nadar aqui (para as crianças)? *eh segooroo nadar akee (parra ash creansash)?*
Are there any currents? ___	Há correntes? *ah coorentesh?*
Are there any rapids/ _____ waterfalls in this river?	Este rio tem rápidos/cataratas? *esht reeoo taim rappeedoosh/cataratash?*

What does that flag/buoy mean?	O que significa aquela bandeira/bóia? *oo kuh signeefeeca akela bandayra/boya?*
Is there a life guard on duty here?	Há aqui um salva-vidas? *ah akee oom salva-veedash?*
Are dogs allowed here?	São permitidos cães aqui? *sow permeeteedoosh caynz akee?*
Is camping on the beach allowed?	Pode-se acampar aqui na praia? *pod suh acampar akee na prya?*
Is it permitted to build a fire here?	Pode-se fazer uma fogueira aqui? *pod suh fazair ooma foogayra akee?*

Perigo **Danger**	É proibido pescar **No fishing**	É proibido nadar **No swimming**
É permitido pescar **Fishing allowed**	É proibido fazer surf **No surfing**	Só com licença **Permits only**

Sickness

13 Sickness

13 .1 Call (fetch) the doctor

Could you call/fetch a_____ doctor quickly, please?
Podia chamar/ir buscar um médico depressa, se faz favor?
poodia shamar/eer booshcar oom maydeecoo, suh faj favvor?

When does the doctor _____ have surgery?
Quando é a consulta do médico?
cuarndoo eh a consoolta doo meydeecoo?

When can the doctor _____ come?
Quando é que o médico pode vir?
cuarndoo eh kuh oo meydeecoo pod veer?

I'd like to make an_____ appointment to see the doctor
Podia marcar-me uma consulta no médico?
poodia marcar muh ooma consoolta noo meydeecoo?

I've got an appointment ___ to see the doctor at...
Tenho uma consulta no médico às...horas
tenyoo ooma consoolta noo meydeecoo az...orash

Which doctor/chemist _____ has night/weekend duty?
Que médico/farmácia tem serviço nocturno/de fim de semana?
kuh meydeecoo/farmassia taim sairveesoo notoornoo/duh feem duh semarna?

13 .2 Patient's ailments

I don't feel well _____
Não me sinto bem
now muh seentoo baim

I'm dizzy_____
Tenho tonturas
tenyoo tontoorash

I feel ill _____
Sinto-me doente
seentoo muh dooent

I feel sick _____
Sinto-me enjoado
seento muh enjooardoo

I've got a cold_____
Sinto-me constipado
seento muh conshteepardoo

It hurts here _____
Dói-me aqui
doy muh akee

I've been throwing up _____
Vomitei
voomeetay

I've got a headache_____
Tenho dor de cabeca
tenyoo door duh cabaysa

I'm running a _____ temperature of...degrees
Tenho...graus de febre
tenyoo...growsh duh febre

I've been stung by_____ a wasp
Fui picado por uma abelha
fwee peecardoo por ooma abelya

I've been stung by an_____ insect
Fui picado por um insecto
fwee picardoo por oom eensetoo

I've been bitten by _____ a dog
Fui mordido por um cão
fwee mordeedoo por oom cow

I've been stung by_____ a jellyfish
Fui mordido por uma alforreca
fwee mordeedoo por ooma alfooreka

I've been bitten by _____ a snake
Fui mordido por uma cobra
fwee mordeedoo por ooma cobbra

I've been bitten by _____ an animal	Fui mordido por um bicho *fwee mordeedoo por oom beeshoo*
I've cut myself _____	Cortei-me *cortay muh*
I've burned myself _____	Queimei-me *kaymay muh*
I've grazed myself_____	Fiz um arranhão *feez oom aranyow*
I've had a fall _____	Caí *ky*
I've sprained my ankle_____	Torci o tornozelo *torsee oo toornnzeloo*
I've come for a _____ morning-after pill	Venho pedir uma pílula `morning-after' *venyoo pedeer ooma peeloola 'morning-after'*

13.3 The consultation

O que tem?_____	What seems to be the problem?
Há quanto tempo sofre disto? _____	How long have you had these symptoms?
Já teve isto antes? _____	Have you had this trouble before?
Que febre tem? _____	How high is your temperature?
Podia despir-se, se faz favor? _____	Get undressed, please
Podia despir-se da cintura para cima? ___	Strip to the waist
Pode despir-se ali_____	You can undress there
Puxe a manga esquerda/direita para ____ cima?	Roll up your left/right sleeve
Deite-se aqui _____	Lie down here
Isto faz-lhe doer? _____	Does this hurt?
Respire fundo _____	Breathe deeply
Abra a boca _____	Open your mouth

Patient's medical history

I'm a diabetic _____	Sofro de diabetes *sofroo duh deeabetsh*
I have a heart condition____	Sofro do coração *sofroo doo coorasow*
I have asthma_____	Sofro de asma *sofroo di ajma*
I'm allergic to... _____	Sou alérgico a... *soe alergeeco ah...*
I'm...months pregnant _____	Estou grávida de...meses *eshtoe graveeda duh...meyzesh*
I'm on a diet _____	Estou de dieta *eshtoe duh deeayta*
I'm on medication/the pill__	Tomo medicamentos/a pílula *tomoo medeecamentoosh/a peeloola*

I've had a heart attack once before	Já tive outro ataque cardíaco *jah teev ohtroo atak cardeeacoo*
I've had a...operation	Fui operado de... *fwee operardoo duh...*
I've been ill recently	Estive doente recentemente *eshteev dooent recentement*
I've got an ulcer	Tenho uma úlcera *tenyoo ooma oolsera*
I've got my period	Estou com a menstruação *eshtoe com a menshtrooasow*

The diagnosis

Is it contagious?	É contagioso? *eh contajiozoo?*
How long do I have to stay...?	Quanto tempo tenho de ficar...? *cuarntoo tempoo tenyoo duh feecar...?*
– in bed	Quanto tempo tenho de ficar de cama? *cuarntoo tempoo tenyoo duh feecar duh camma?*
– in hospital	Quanto tempo tenho de ficar no hospital? *cuarntoo tempoo tenyoo duh feecar noo oshpeetal?*

É alérgico a qualquer coisa?	Do you have any allergies?
Toma medicamentos?	Are you on any medication?
Faz qualquer dieta?	Are you on any sort of diet?
Está grávida?	Are you pregnant?
Está vacinado contra o tétano?	Have you had a tetanus vaccination?
Não é nada de grave	It's nothing serious
Partiu o/a...	You've broken your...
Magoou o/a...	You've bruised your...
Estalou o/a...	You've split your...
Tem uma inflamação	You've got an inflammation
Tem uma apendicite	You've got appendicitis
Tem uma bronquite	You've got bronchitis
Tem uma doença venérea	You've got a venereal disease
Tem uma gripe	You've got the flu
Teve um ataque cardíaco	You've had a heart attack
Tem uma infecção (provocada por um vírus/uma bactéria)	You've got an infection (viral/bacteria)
Tem uma infecção pulmonar	You've got pneumonia
Tem uma úlcera	You've got an ulcer
Distendeu um músculo	You've pulled a muscle
Tem uma infecção na vagina	You've got a vaginal infection
Tem uma intoxicação de alimentos	You've got food poisoning

Sickness

13

Apanhou uma insolação _____	You've got sunstroke
É alérgico a... _____	You're allergic to...
Está grávida _____	You're pregnant
Tem de fazer análises ao sangue/à ___ urina/às fezes	You'll need to have your blood/urine/stools tested
Tem de levar pontos _____	It needs stitching
Tem de ir a um especialista/para o ___ hospital	I'm referring you to a specialist/sending you to hospital
Tem de tirar radiografias _____	You'll need to have some x-rays taken
Pode aguardar ainda na sala de espera, se faz favor? _____	Could you wait in the waiting room, please?
Tem de ser operado _____	You'll need an operation

Do I have to go on a special diet? _____	Tenho de fazer alguma dieta? *tenyoo duh fazair algooma diayta?*
Am I allowed to travel? ___	Posso viajar? *possoo veajar?*
Can I make a new appointment? _____	Posso marcar outra consulta? *possoo marcar ohtra conssoolta?*
When do I have to come back? _____	Quando é que tenho de voltar? *cuarndoo eh kuh tenyoo duh voltar?*
I'll come back tomorrow _____	Volto amanhã *voltoo armanyar*

Volte amanhã/daqui a...dias _____	Come back tomorrow/in...days' time

📞 .4 Medication and prescriptions

How do I take this medicine? _____	Como é que tenho de tomar este medicamento? *coemoo eh kuh tenyoo duh toomar esht medeecamentoo?*
How many capsules/ drops/injections/ spoonfuls/tablets each time? _____	Quantas cápsulas/gotas/injecções/ colheres/comprimidos de uma vez? *cuarntash capsoolash/gottash, eenjecsoynsh/coolyairesh/compreemeedo sh di ooma vej?*
How many times a day? ___	Quantas vezes por dia? *cuarntash vayzesh por deeah?*
I've forgotten my medication. At home I take...	Esqueci-me dos meus medicamentos. Costumo tomar... *eshkesee muh doosh mayoosh meydeecamentoosh. coshtoomoo toomar...*
Could you make out a prescription for me? _____	Podia passar-me uma receita? *poodia passar muh ooma ressayta?*

Receito-lhe um antibiótico/xarope/ _____ sedativo/analgésico	I'm prescribing antibiotics/a mixture/a tranquillizer/pain killers
Tem de descansar_____	You need to rest
Tem de ficar dentro de casa _____	Stay indoors
Tem de ficar na cama _____	Stay in bed

antes das refeições before meals	durante...dias for...days	só para uso externo only for external use
cápsulas capsules	engolir inteiro swallow whole	terminar a cura finish the prescription
dissolver em água dissolve in water	esfregar rub on	tomar take
comprimidos tablets	gotas drops	este medicamento pode influenciar a condução
colheres (de sopa/de chá) spoonfuls (tablespoons/ teaspoons)	injecções injections	this medication impairs your driving
	pomada ointment	
	...vezes por dia ...times a day	

🖐️ .5 At the dentist's

Do you know a good _____ dentist?	Conhece um bom dentista? *coonyess oom bom denteeshta?*
Could you make a _____ dentist's appointment for me? It's urgent	Podia marcar-me uma consulta no dentista? É urgente *poodia marcar muh ooma consoolta noo denteeshta? Eh oorgent*
Can I come in today,_____ please?	Podia ser ainda hoje? *poodia sair ayeenda oarje?*
I have (terrible)_____ toothache	Tenho (imensa) dor de dentes *tenyoo (eemensa) door duh dentesh*
Could you prescribe/ _____ give me a painkiller?	Podia receitar-me um analgésico? *poodia ressaytar muh oom analjezzeecoo?*
One of my teeth_____ has cracked	Partiu-se um dos meus dentes *partyoo suh oom doosh mayoosh dentesh*
My filling's come out _____	O chumbo do dente caiu *oo choomboo doo dent cayoo*
I've got a cracked crown ___	Partiu-se a coroa *partyoo suh ah coroah*
I'd like/I don't want a _____ local anaesthetic	Gostava/não gostava de anestesia local *goshtarv/now goshtarv duh aneshtezia loocal*
Can you do a makeshift____ repair job?	Podia fazer um arranjo provisório? *poodia fazair oom arranjoo prooveesoryoo?*
I don't want this tooth ____ pulled	Não quero que arranque este dente *now cairoo kuh arrank esht dent*

Sickness

13

My dentures are broken.___ A minha dentadura partiu-se.
  Can you fix them?   Podia arranjá-la?
                     a meenya dentadoora partyoo suh.
                     Poodia arranjar la?

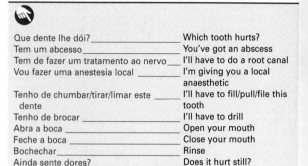

Que dente lhe dói?_____	Which tooth hurts?
Tem um abcesso_____	You've got an abscess
Tem de fazer um tratamento ao nervo___	I'll have to do a root canal
Vou fazer uma anestesia local _____	I'm giving you a local anaesthetic
Tenho de chumbar/tirar/limar este ____ dente	I'll have to fill/pull/file this tooth
Tenho de brocar _____	I'll have to drill
Abra a boca _____	Open your mouth
Feche a boca _____	Close your mouth
Bochechar_____	Rinse
Ainda sente dores? _____	Does it hurt still?

13 Sickness

In trouble

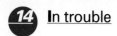

14 In trouble

14.1 Asking for help

Help!	Socorro! *socooroo!*
Fire!	Fogo! *foegoo!*
Police!	Polícia! *pooleecia!*
Quick!	Depressa! *depressa!*
Danger!	Perigo! *pereegoo!*
Watch out!	Atenção! *atensow*
Stop!	Páre! *parah!*
Be careful!	Cuidado! *cweedardoo*
Don't!	Não faça isso! *now fassa eessoo!*
Let go!	Largar! *largar!*
Stop that thief!	Apanhe o ladrão! *apanya oo ladrow!*
Could you help me, please?	Podia ajudar-me? *poodia ajoodar muh?*
Where's the police station/emergency exit/fire escape?	Onde é a polícia/a saída de emergência/a escada de incêndios? *ond eh a pooleecia/a sayeeda di emerjencia/a eshcarda di eencendyoosh?*
Where's the nearest fire extinguisher?	Onde está o extintor? *ond eshtah oo eshteentor?*
Call the fire brigade!	Chame os bombeiros! *shamma oosh bombayroosh!*
Call the police!	Telefone à polícia *telefon ah pooleecia!*
Call an ambulance!	Chame uma ambulância *shamma ooma amboolancia*
Where's the nearest phone?	Onde é o telefone? *ond eh oo telefon?*
Could I use your phone?	Posso usar o seu telefone? *possoo oozar oo sayoo telefon?*
What's the emergency number?	Qual é o número de urgência? *cuarl eh oo noomeroo duh oorjensia?*
What's the number for the police?	Qual é o número da polícia? *cuarl eh oo noomeroo da pooleecia?*

14.2 Loss

I've lost my purse/_____ | Perdi o meu porta-moedas/a minha
wallet | carteira
  | *pairdee oo mayoo porta mooaydash/a*
  | *meenya cartayra*
I lost my...yesterday _____ | Ontem esqueci-me do meu/da minha...
  | *ontaim eshkecee muh doo mayoo/da*
  | *meenya...*
I left my...here _____ | Deixei aqui o meu/a minha...
  | *dayshay akee oo mayoo/a meenya...*
Did you find my...? _____ | Encontrou o meu/a minha...?
  | *encontroe oo mayoo/a meenya...?*
It was right here_____ | Estava aqui
  | *eshtarva akee*
It's quite valuable _____ | É bastante valioso
  | *eh bashtant valiozoo*
Where's the lost_____ | Onde é a secção de perdidos e
property office? | achados?
  | *ond eh a seksow duh pairdeedoos e*
  | *achardoosh?*

14.3 Accidents

There's been an accident __ | Houve um acidente
  | *ohve oom asseedent*
Someone's fallen into _____ | Caiu uma pessoa na água
the water | *cayoo ooma pessoa nah agwa*
There's a fire_____ | Há fogo
  | *ha foegoo*
Is anyone hurt? _____ | Alguém está ferido?
  | *algaim eshtah fereedoo?*
No one's been injured _____ | Não há feridos
  | *now ah fereedoosh*
Some people have been ___ | Há alguns feridos
injured | *ah algoons fereedoosh*
There's still someone in ___ | Ainda há uma pessoa no carro/comboio
the car/train | *ayeenda hah ooma pessoa noo*
  | *cahroo/comboyoo*
It's not too bad. Don't_____ | Não é nada. Não se preocupe
worry | *now eh narda. Now suh preeocoop*
Don't touch anything _____ | Não mexa em nada
  | *now mesha aim narda*
I want to talk to the_____ | Queria falar primeiro com a polícia
police first | *kerria falar preemayroo com a pooleecia*
I want to take a _____ | Primeiro quero tirar uma fotografia
photo first | *preemayroo cairoo teerar ooma*
  | *fotografeea*
Here's my name_____ | Tem aqui o meu nome e morada
and address | *taim akee oo mayoo nom ee moorarda*
Could I have your _____ | Podia dar-me o seu nome e morada?
name and address? | *poodia dar muh oo sayoo nom e*
  | *moorarda?*
Could I see some_____ | Posso ver os seus documentos de
identification/your | identificação/o seu seguro?
insurance papers? | *possoo vair oosh sayoosh docoomentoosh*
  | *di eedentifeecasow/oo sayoo segooroo?*

In trouble

107

Will you act as a _____ witness?	Quer ser testemunha?
	care sair teshtemoonya?
I need to know the details__ for the insurance	Tenho de saber os dados para o seguro
	tenyoo duh sabbair oosh dardoosh parra oo segooroo
Are you insured? _____	Tem um seguro?
	taim oom segooroo?
Third party or _____ comprehensive?	Contra terceiros ou contra todos os riscos?
	contra tairsayroosh o contra toedoos oosh reeshcoosh?
Could you sign here, _____ please?	Podia assinar aqui?
	poodia asseenar akee?

🔴 .4 Theft

I've been robbed _____	Fui roubado
	fwee roobardoo
My...has been stolen _____	Roubaram-me o meu/a minha...
	roobaram muh oo mayoo/a meenya...
My car's been _____ broken into	Assaltaram-me o carro
	assalltaram muh oo cahroo

🔴 .5 Missing person

I've lost my child/ _____ grandmother	Perdi o meu filho (a minha filha)/a minha avó
	pairdee oo mayoo feelyoo (a meenya feelya)/a meenya avoh
Could you help me _____ find him/her?	Podia ajudar-me a procurar?
	poodia ajoodar muh a procoorar?
Have you seen a _____ small child?	Viu uma criança pequena?
	veeoo ooma creeansa peekayna?
He's/she's...years old _____	Ele/ela tem...anos
	el/alla taim...arnoosh
He's/she's got _____ short/long/blond/red/ brown/black/grey/ straight/curly/frizzy hair	Ele/ela tem cabelo curto/comprido/louro/ ruivo/castanho/preto/grisalho/liso/ encaracolado/frizado
	el/ella taim cabayloo coortoo/rooeevoo/cashtanyoo/ praytoo/greesalyoo/leezoo/ aincarracoolardoo/freezardoo
in a ponytail _____	tem rabo de cavalo
	taim rarboo duh cavarloo
in plaits_____	tem tranças
	taim transash
in a bun _____	tem um carrapito
	taim oom carrapeetoo
He's/she's got _____ blue/brown/green eyes	Os olhos são azuis/castanhos/verdes
	ooz olyoosh sow azweesh/castanyoosh/vairdsh
He's wearing swimming ___ trunks/mountaineering boots	Tem uns calções de banho vestidos/uns sapatos de alpinismo calçados
	taim unsh calsoynsh de bahnyoo veshteedoosh/unsh sapartoosh di alpeeneejmoo calsardoosh

with/without glasses/ _____ a bag	com/sem óculos/saco *com/saim occooloosh/sarcoo*
tall/short _____	grande/pequeno *grand/peekaynoo*
This is a photo of _____ him/her	Esta fotografia é dele/dela *eshta fotoografeea eh del/della*
He/she must be lost _____	Com certeza ele/ela se perdeu *com sairtayza el/ella suh pairdayoo*

14 .6 The police

An arrest

I don't speak Portuguese _____	Não falo português *now faloo poortoogayj*
I didn't see that sign _____	Não vi aquele sinal *now vee akel seenal*
I don't understand _____ what it says	Não compreendo o que significa *now comprayendoo oo kuh seegneefeeca*
I was only doing... _____ kilometres an hour	Só vinha a...km por hora *soh veenya a...km poor ora*
I'll have my car checked _____	Vou levar o meu carro à oficina *voe levvar oo mayoo cahro ah offeeseena*
I was blinded by _____ oncoming lights	Fiquei encadeado pelos faróis em sentido contrário *feekay encaddeardoo peloosh faroysh aim senteedoo contraryoo*

Os seus documentos, se faz favor _____	Your registration papers, please
Excedeu a velocidade máxima _____	You were speeding
Está mal estacionado _____	You're not allowed to park here
Não pôs dinheiro no parquímetro _____	You haven't put money in the meter
As luzes não funcionam _____	Your lights aren't working
É uma multa de...escudos _____	That's a...escudos fine
Quer pagar agora? _____	Do you want to pay on the spot?
Tem de pagar agora _____	You'll have to pay on the spot

At the police station

I want to report a _____ collision/missing person/rape	Venho declarar uma colisão/um desaparecimento/uma violação *venyoo declarar ooma cooleesow/oom dezaparessimentoo/ooma veeoolasow*
Could you make out _____ a report, please?	Podia fazer um relatório, se faz favor? *poodia fazair oom relatoryoo, suh faj favvor?*
Could I have a copy _____ for the insurance?	Posso levar uma cópia para o seguro? *possoo levvar ooma copia parra oo segooroo?*

I've lost everything _____ Perdi tudo
pairdee toodoo

I've no money at all. _____ Não tenho dinheiro nenhum. Estou
I'm desperate desesperado
now tenyoo deenyayroo nenyoom. eshtoe deseshperardoo

Can you lend me some ____ Pode emprestar-me algum dinheiro?
money? *poodia empreshtar muh algoom deenyayroo?*

I'd like an interpreter _____ Queria um intérprete
kerria oom eentairpret

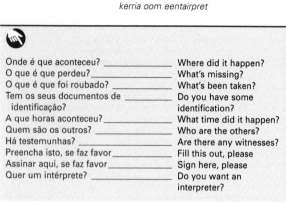

Onde é que aconteceu? _____ Where did it happen?
O que é que perdeu? _____ What's missing?
O que é que foi roubado? _____ What's been taken?
Tem os seus documentos de _____ Do you have some
identificação? identification?
A que horas aconteceu? _____ What time did it happen?
Quem são os outros? _____ Who are the others?
Há testemunhas? _____ Are there any witnesses?
Preencha isto, se faz favor _____ Fill this out, please
Assinar aqui, se faz favor _____ Sign here, please
Quer um intérprete? _____ Do you want an
interpreter?

I'm innocent _____ Estou inocente
eshtoe eenoosent

I don't know anything ____ Não sei nada
about it *now say narda*

I want to speak to _____ Queria falar com alguém do Consulado
someone from the Británico
British consulate *kerria falar com algaim doo consoolardoo breetaneecoo*

I want to speak to _____ Queria falar com alguém da Embaixada
someone from the Británica
British embassy *kerria falar com algaim da embysharda breetaneeca*

I want a lawyer_____ Queria um advogado que fale inglês
who speaks English *kerria oom advoogardoo kuh fal eenglayj*

In trouble

14

15

Word list

Word list English - Portuguese

● **This word list** is meant to supplement previous chapters.
In a number of cases, words not contained in this list can be found
elsewhere in this book, namely alongside the diagrams of the car, the
bicycle and the tent. Many food terms can be found in the
Portuguese-English list in 4.7

A

about	acerca de	asserca duh
above, up	em cima	aim seema
abroad	estrangeiro	eshtranjayroo
accident	acidente	assident
adder	víbora	veebora
addition	soma	somma
address	morada	mooradah
adhesive tape	fita cola	feeta colla
admission	entrada	entrarda
admission price	preço de entrada	praysoo duh entrarda
advice	conselho	consellyoo
after	depois	depoysh
afternoon	tarde	tard
aftershave	loção para a barba	loosow parra ah barba
again	novamente	novvament
against	contra	contra
age	idade	eedarde
Aids	Sida	seeda
air conditioning	ar condicionado	ar condeesionardoo
air mattress	colchão inflável	colchow eenflarvel
air sickness bag	saco para enjôo	sarcoo parra ainjoh-oo
aircraft	avião	avviow
airport	aeroporto	airoopoortoo
alarm	alarme	alarm
alarm clock	despertador	deshpairtadoor
alcohol	âlcool	alcoooll
allergic	alérgico	alergeecoo
alone	só	soh
always	sempre	sempra
ambulance	ambulância	amboolancia
amount	quantia, quantidade	quarnteeah, quarnteedard
amusement park	parque de diversões	park duh deevaisoynsh
anaesthetize	anestesiar	aneshteziar
anchovy	anchovas	anshovvash
angry	zangado	zangardoo
animal	animal	animarl
ankle	tornozelo	tornoozelloo
answer	resposta	reshposhta
ant	formiga	formeega
antibiotics	antibióticos	antibeeoteecoosh
antifreeze	anticongelante	anticongellant
antique	antigo	anteegoo
antiques	antiguidades	anteegweedardesh
anus	ânus	arnoosh
apartment	apartamento	apartamentoo
aperitif	aperitivo	aperiteevoo
apologies	desculpas	descoolpash
apple	maçã	massar

apple juice	sumo de maçã	*soomoo duh massar*
apple pie	tarte de maçã	*tarte duh massar*
appointment	consulta	*consoolta*
apricot	alperce	*alpairce*
April	abril	*abreel*
architecture	arquitectura	*arkeetetoora*
area	arredores	*arredoresh*
arm	braço	*brarsoo*
arrange	combinar	*combeenar*
arrive	chegar	*sheggar*
arrow	seta	*setta*
art	arte	*art*
artery	artéria	*arterrya*
artichokes	alcachofras	*alcashoffrash*
article	artigo	*arteegoo*
artificial respiration	respiração artificial	*reshpeerasow arteefeecial*
ashtray	cinzeiro	*seenzayroo*
ask	perguntar	*pairgoontar*
ask	pedir	*pedeer*
asparagus	espargos	*eshpargoosh*
aspirin	aspirina	*ashpeereena*
assault	assalto	*assaltoo*
at home	em casa	*aim carza*
at last	afinal	*afeenal*
at night	à noite	*ah noyt*
at the back	atrás	*atraj*
at the front	à frente	*ah frent*
at the latest	no mais tardar	*noo mysh tardar*
aubergine	beringela	*berringella*
August	agosto	*agoshtoo*
automatic	automático	*owtoomateecoo*
automatically	automaticamente	*owtoomateecament*
autumn	outono	*ohtonoo*
awake	acordado	*acordardoo*
awning	toldo	*toldoo*

B

baby's bottle	biberão	*beeberow*
baby	bebé	*baybay*
baby car-seat	cadeira para bébé	*caddayra parra baybay*
baby food	comida para bébé	*comeeda parra baybay*
babysitter	babysitter	*baybeeseetair*
back	costas	*coshtash*
bacon	toucinho	*toosseenyoo*
bad	mau	*mow*
bad/off	estragado	*eshtragardoo*
bag (plastic)	saco (de plástico)	*sarcoo duh plashteecoo*
baker	padeiro	*paddayroo*
balcony (theatre)	balcão	*balcow*
balcony (of building)	varanda	*varanda*
ball	bola	*bolla*
ballet	ballet	*ballay*
ballpoint pen	esferográfica	*eshferoografeeca*
banana	banana	*bananna*
bandage	ligadura	*leegadoura*
bank (river)	margem	*marjaim*
bank	banco	*bancoo*

bar (café)	café	cafay
bar (drinks' cabinet)	bar	bar
barbecue	churrasco	shoorashcoo
bath	banho	barnyoo
bath foam	espuma de banho	eshpooma duh barnyoo
bath towel	toalha de banho	tooalya duh barnyoo
bath-tub	banheira	banyayra
bathing cap	touca de banho	toeca duh barnyoo
bathing suit	fato de banho	fartoo duh barnyoo
bathroom	casa de banho	carza duh banyoo
battery	pilha	peelya
battery	bateria	batareeya
be bored	aborrecer-se	abooressair-suh
be careful!	cuidado!	cweedardoo
be foggy	fazer nevoeiro	fazzair nevooayroo
be hungry	ter fome	tair fom
be in love with	estar namorado com	eshtar namorardoo com
be lost	perder-se	pairdair-se
be missing	faltar	faltar
be mistaken	enganar-se	ainganar-suh
beach	praia	prya
beautiful	lindo/belo	leendoo/ bella
beauty parlour	salão de beleza	salow duh bellayza
bed	cama	camma
bee	abelha	abellya
beef	carne de vaca	carn duh varca
beer	cerveja	sairvayja
beetroot	beterraba	betterrarb
begin	começar	coomessar
beginner	principiante	preenseepeeant
behind	atrás	atraj
belt	cinto	seentoo
beret	boina	booeena
berth	couchete	cooshet
better	melhor	melyor
bicarbonate of soda	bicarbonato de sódio	beecarboonartoo duh sohdew
bicycle	bicicleta	beeseecletta
bicycle pump	bomba de bicicleta	bomba duh beeseecletta
bicycle repair workshop	oficina de bicicletas	offiseena duh beeseeclettash
bikini	biquini	bee-kee-nee
bill	conta	conta
billiards, to play	jogar bilhar	joogar beelyar
birthday	aniversário	anneevairsareeyoo
birthday, to have a...	fazer anos	fazzair arnoosh
biscuit	biscoito	beeshcoytoo
bite	morder	mordair
bitter	amargo	amargoo
black	preto	pretoo
bland	insêpido	eenseepeedoo
blanket	cobertor	coobertor
bleach (hair)	pintar de louro	peentar duh loroo
bleeding nose	deitar sangue pelo nariz	daytar sang peloo nareej
blister	bolha	bolya
blond	louro	loroo

blood	sangue	*sang*
blood pressure	tensão arterial	*tensow arterrial*
blouse	blusa	*blooza*
blow dry	secar	*seccar*
blue	azul	*azool*
boat	barco	*barcoo*
body	corpo	*corpoo*
body milk	leite de beleza	*layt duh bellayza*
boiled	cozido	*coozeedoo*
boiled ham	fiambre	*feeambr*
bonbon	bombom	*bombom*
bone	osso	*ossoo*
bonnet	tampa do motor	*tampa doo motor*
book	livro	*leevroo*
book	reservar	*reservar*
booked	reservado	*reservardoo*
booking office	bilheteria	*beelyetareeah*
bookshop	livraria	*leevrareeah*
border	fronteira	*frontayra*
boring	monótono	*monotoonoo*
born/be born	nascido/nascer	*nashseedoo/nashayr*
borrow	pedir emprestado	*pedeer aimpreshtardoo*
botanical garden	jardim botânico	*jardeem bootaneecoo*
both	ambos	*amboosh*
bottlewarmer	aquecedor de biberões	*akessedor duh beeberoynsh*
bottle	garrafa	*garraffa*
box	caixa	*kysha*
box (theatre)	camarote	*cammarot*
boy	rapaz	*rapaj*
bra	soutien	*sootyan*
bracelet	pulseira	*poolsayra*
braised	estufado	*eshtoofardoo*
brake	travão	*travow*
brake fluid	líquido de travões	*leekeedoo duh travoynsh*
brake oil	óleo dos travões	*ollyoo doosh travoynsh*
brass	latão	*latow*
bread	pão	*pow*
break	partir	*parteer*
break-down	avaria do motor	*avaria doo motor*
breakdown service	pronto socorro	*prontoo socorroo*
breakfast	pequeno almoço	*peekaynoo almossoo*
breast	peito	*paytoo*
bridge	ponte	*pont*
bring	trazer	*trazair*
brochure	brochura	*brooshura*
broken	estragado	*eshtragardoo*
broken	partido	*parteedoo*
broth	caldo	*caldoo*
brother	irmão	*irmow*
brown	castanho	*cashtanyoo*
bruise	magoar	*magooar*
brush	escova	*eshcova*
bucket	balde	*balde*
bug	bicho	*beeshoo*
bugs	insectos	*eensetoosh*
building	edifício	*eedifeesyoo*

buoy	bóia	boya
bureau de change	casa de câmbio	caza duh cambyoo
burglary	assalto	assaltoo
burn	queimar	kaymar
burn	queimadura	kaymadoora
burnt	queimado	kaymardoo
bus station	estação de camionetas	eshtasow duh camyoonetash
bus stop	paragem de autocarro	pararjaim duh owtoocahroo
bus, coach	autocarro	owtoocahroo
business class	classe de negócios	class duh negossyoosh
business trip	viagem de negócios	veearjaim duh negossioosh
busy	atarefado/ocupado	atarrefardoo/okoopardoo
butcher	talho	talyoo
butter	manteiga	mantayga
buttered roll	pãozinho (com manteiga)	powzeenyoo (com mantayga)
button	botão	bootow
buy	comprar	comprar
by airmail	por correio aéreo	por coorayoo airayoo

C

cabbage	couve	cove
cabin on ship	camarote	camarot
café	café	cafay
cake	bolinho	boleenyoo
cake	bolo	boloo
cake shop	pastelaria	pastellereeah
call	telefonar	telefoonar
called, to be	chamar-se	shammar-suh
camera	máquina fotográfica	markeena fotografeeca
camp	acampar	acampar
camp shop	loja	lohja
camp site	campismo	campeejmoo
camp site	parque de campismo	park duh campeejmoo
camp-fire	fogueira	foogayra
camper	carrinha de campismo	careenya duh campeejmoo
camping guide	guia de campismo	gueeah duh campeejmoo
camping permit	autorização de campismo	owtoreezasow duh campeejmoo
canal boat	barco de excursão	barcoo di eshcoorsow
cancel	anular	anoolar
candle	vela	vella
canoe	canoa	canoah
canoe	fazer canoagem	fazzair canooarjaim
car	automóvel	owtoomohvel
car	carruagem	carruarjaim
car deck	porão de veículos	poorow duh vayeecooloosh
car documents	documentos do carro	docoomentoosh doo cahroo
caravan	roulotte	roolott
cardigan	casaco	cazarcoo
carrot	cenoura	senora

cartridge	carga de película fotogrâfica	carga duh peleecoola fottoograrfeeca
cash desk	caixa	kysha
casino	casino	cazzeenoo
cassette	cassette	cassett
castle	castelo	cashteloo
cat	gato	gartoo
catalogue	catálogo	catalogoo
cathedral	catedral	cataydral
cauliflower	couveflor	cove flor
cave	gruta	groota
CD	disco compacto (CD)	deeshcoo compactoo (sayday)
celebrate	festejar	feshtayjar
cemetery	cemitério	semmeeterryoo
centimetre	centímetro	senteemetroo
central heating	aquecimento central (no) meio	akessimento centrarl (noo) mayoo
centre	centro	centroo
chair	cadeira	cadayra
chambermaid	camareira	camarayra
champagne	champanhe	shampanya
change	alterar	alterrar
change	mudar	moodar
change (transit)	fazer transbordo	fazzair transhbordoo
change	trocar	troocar
change currency	trocar dinheiro	troocar deenyayroo
change the baby's nappy	mudar a fralda	moodar ah fralda
change the oil	mudar o óleo	moodar oo ollyoo
chapel	capela	capella
charter flight	vôo charter	voe shartair
chat up	paquerar	pakerrar
check	ver, controlar	vair, comtroolar
check in	fazer o checkin	fazzair oo sheckeen
cheers	à saúde	ah sow-ood
cheese (tasty, mild)	queijo (bem curado, mal curado)	kayjoo (baim coorardoo, mal coorardoo)
chef	cozinheiro-chefe	coozeenyayroo chef
chemist	farmácia	farmassia
cheque	cheque	sheck
cheque card	cartão de cheques	cartow duh sheksh
cherries	cerejas	serayjash
chess, play	jogar xadrez	joogar jadrayj
chewing gum	pastilha elástica/ chiclete	pashteelya eelashteeca/ cheeclet
chicken	galinha, frango	galeenya, frangoo
child	criança	creeansa
child's seat	cadeira para bicicleta	cadayra parra beeseecletta
chilled	fresco	freshcoo
chin	queixo	kayshoo
chips	batatas fritas	batartash freetash
chocolate	chocolate	shoocoolat
choose	escolher	eschoolyair
chop	costeleta	coshteletta
christian name	nome	nom
church	igreja	eegrayja

church service	missa	meessa
cigar	charuto	charootoo
cigar shop	tabacaria	tabacareeah
cigarette	cigarro	seegarroo
circle	círculo	seercooloo
circus	circo	seercoo
city	cidade	seedard
city map	planta da cidade	planta da seedard
classical concert	concerto de música clássica	consairtoo duh mooseeca classeeca
clean	limpo	leempoo
clean, to	limpar	leempar
clearance	saldo	saldoo
closed	fechado	feshardoo
clothes	roupa	roepa
clothes hanger	cabide	cabeed
clothes pegs	molas para a roupa	mollas parra ah roepa
clothing	vestuário	veshtooaryoo
coat	casaco	cazarcoo
cockroach	barata	barata
cocoa	cacau	cackow
cod	bacalhau fresco	bacalyow freshcoo
coffee	café	cafay
coffee filter	filtro de café	feeltroo duh cafay
cognac	conhaque	coonyack
cold (to be)	frio	freeoo
cold (to have a)	constipação	conshteepasow
collarbone	clavícula	claveecoola
colleague	colega	coolegga
collision	acidente	asseedent
collision	colisão	cooleezow
cologne	água de colônia	agwa duh collonia
colour	cor	cor
colour pencils	lápis de cor	larpeej duh coor
colour TV	televisão a cores	televeesow ah cooresh
colouring book	livro para colorir	leevroo parra coloreer
comb	pente	pent
come	vir	veer
come back	regressar, voltar	regressar, voltar
compartment	compartimento	compartimentoo
complaint	dor	door
complaint	queixa	kaysha
complaints book	livro de reclamações	leevroo duh reclammasoynsh
completely	completamente	completament
compliment	cumprimento	coomprimentoo
compulsory	obrigatório	obrigatoryoo
concert	concerto	consairtoo
concert hall, theatre	teatro	teeartroo
concussion	concussão cerebral	concoosow cerebral
condensed milk	leite condensado	layt condensardoo
condom	preservativo	presairvateevoo
congratulate	felicitar	feleeceetar
connection	ligação	leegasow
constipation	prisão de ventre	preezow duh ventre
consulate	consulado	consoolardoo
consultation	consulta	consoolta

contact lens	lente de contacto	*lent duh contactoo*
contact lens solution	fluido para lentes de contacto	*flooidoo parra lentsh duh contactoo*
contagious	contagioso	*contajeeozoo*
contraceptive pill	pílula anticoncepcional	*peeloola anttconcepseeoonarl*
cook	cozinheiro	*coozeenyayroo*
cook, to	cozinhar	*coozeenyar*
copper	cobre	*cobbre*
copy	cópia	*cohpia*
corkscrew	sacarolhas	*sacca rollyash*
corn flour	maizena	*myzenna*
corner	canto	*cantoo*
corner	esquina	*eshkeena*
correct	certo	*sairtoo*
correspond	corresponder	*cooreshpondair*
corridor	corredor	*cooredoor*
cot	cama de bebé	*camma duh baybay*
cotton	algodão	*algoodow*
cotton wool	algodão	*algoodow*
cough	tosse	*toss*
cough mixture	xarope para a tosse	*sharopp parra a toss*
country	país	*pyeej*
country	campoo	*campoo*
country code	indicativo do país	*eendeecateevoo*
courgette	courgete	*corjet*
cousin	primo/prima	*preemoo/preema*
crab	caranguejo	*carangayjoo*
cream	creme/natas	*crem/nartash*
credit card	cartão de crédito	*cartow duh credeetoo*
crisps	batatas fritas	*batartash freetash*
croissant	croissant	*croisson*
cross (the road)	atravessar	*atravessar*
crossing	travessia	*travessia*
crossing	passagem	*passarjaim*
cry	chorar	*shoorar*
cubic metre	metro cúbico	*metroo coobeecoo*
cucumber	pepino	*pepeenoo*
cuddly toy	boneco de peluche	*booneckoo duh peloosh*
cuff links	botões de punho	*bootoynsh duh poonyoo*
culottes	saia calça	*syah calsa*
cup	chávena	*sharvena*
curly	encaracolado	*aincarracoolardoo*
current	corrente	*coorent*
cushion	almofadinha	*almoffardeenya*
custard	creme	*crem*
customary	ê costume	*eh coshtoom*
customs	alfândega	*alfandegga*
customs	controle de alfândega	*controll di alfandegga*
cut	cortar	*cortar*
cutlery	talher	*talyair*
cycling	ciclismo	*seecleejmoo*

Word list

15

119

D

English	Portuguese	Pronunciation
dairy	leiteria	*laytereeah*
damaged	danificado	*danifeecardoo*
dance	dançar	*dansar*
dandruff	caspa	*cashpa*
danger	perigo	*perreegoo*
dangerous	perigoso	*perrigozoo*
dark	escuro	*eshcooroo*
date	encontro	*aincontroo*
daughter	filha	*feelya*
day	dia	*deeah*
day before yesterday	anteontem	*antiontaim*
dead	morto	*mortoo*
decaffeinated	descafeinado	*deshcafaynardoo*
December	dezembro	*dezembroo*
deck chair	cadeira de praia	*cadayra duh prya*
declare (customs)	declarar	*declarar*
deep	profundo	*proofoondoo*
deep sea diving	mergulho	*mairgoolyoo*
deepfreeze	congelador	*conjellador*
degrees	graus	*graush*
delay	atraso	*atrarzoo*
delicatessen	charcutaria	*sharcootareeah*
delicious	saboroso	*saborohzoo*
delicious	delicioso	*delisseeohzoo*
dentist	dentista	*denteeshta*
dentures	dentadura	*dentadoora*
deodorant	desodorizante	*desodoreezant*
department	secção	*secksow*
department store	armazém	*armazaim*
departure	partida	*parteeda*
departure time	hora de partida	*ora duh parteeda*
depilatory cream	creme depilatório	*crem depeelatoryoo*
deposit	sinal	*seenal*
dessert	sobremesa	*sobremayza*
destination	destino	*deshteenoo*
destiny	destino	*deshteenoo*
develop	revelar	*revelar*
diabetic	diabético	*deeabeteecoo*
dial	marcar	*marcar*
dialling code	indicativo	*eendeecateevoo*
diamond	diamante	*deeamant*
diarrhoea	diarreia	*deearraya*
dictionary	dicionário	*deesionaryoo*
diesel	diesel	*deezel*
diesel oil	gasóleo	*gazollyoo*
diet	dieta	*deeayta*
difficulty	dificuldade	*deefeeculdard*
dining room	sala de jantar	*sarla duh jantar*
dining/buffet car	vagão restaurante	*vagow reshtowrant*
dinner	jantar	*jantar*
dinner jacket	smoking	*smockeeng*
direction	direcção	*deeressow*
directly	directo	*deerectoo*
dirty	sujo	*soojoo*
disabled	inválido	*eenvalleedoo*
disco	discoteca	*deeshcooteca*

15 Word list

discount	desconto	*deshcontoo*
dish	prato	*prartoo*
dish of the day	prato do dia	*prartoo doo deeah*
disinfectant	desinfectante	*dezeenfectant*
distance	distância	*deeshtarncia*
distilled water	água destilada	*agwa deshteelarda*
disturb	incomodar	*eencoomoodar*
disturbance	perturbação	*pairtoorbasow*
diving	mergulhar	*mairgoolyar*
diving board	prancha de saltos	*pransha duh saltoosh*
diving gear	equipamento para mergulhar	*ekeepamentoo parra mairgoolyar*
divorced	divorciado	*deevorceeardoo*
DIY shop	loja faça-você-mesmo	*loja fassa vossay mejmoo*
dizzy	tonto	*tontoo*
do	fazer	*fazzair*
doctor	médico	*mehdeecoo*
dog	cão	*cow*
doll	boneca	*booneca*
domestic	doméstico	*doomehsteecoo*
door	porta	*porta*
double bed	cama de casal	*camma duh cazal*
down	em baixo	*aim byshoo*
draught	corrente de ar	*coorent di ar*
dream	sonhar	*soonyar*
dress	vestido	*veshteedoo*
dressing gown	roupão	*roepow*
drink	bebida	*bebbeeda*
drink	beber	*bebbair*
drinking chocolate	leite com chocolate	*layt com shoocoolat*
drinking water	água potável	*agwa pootarvel*
drive	conduzir	*condoozeer*
drive	motorista	*motoreeshta*
driving licence	carta de condução	*carta duh condoosow*
drought	seca	*sayca*
dry	secar	*seccar*
dry	seco	*saycoo*
dry clean	limpar a seco	*leempar ah saycoo*
dry cleaner's	limpeza a seco	*leempayza ah saycoo*
dry shampoo	champô seco	*shampoh saycoo*
dummy	chupeta	*shoopeta*
during	durante	*doorant*
during the day	durante o dia	*doorant oo deeah*
duty free shop	loja franca	*loja franca*

E

ear	orelha/ouvido	*orelya/ohveedoo*
ear, nose and throat specialist	otorrinolaringo-logista	*otorreenoolareengoloo-jeeshta*
earache	dor de ouvidos	*door duh oeveedoosh*
eardrops	gotas para os ouvidos	*gotash parra ooz oeveedoosh*
early	cedo	*saydoo*
earrings	brincos	*breencoosh*
earth	terra	*tehrah*
earthenware	cerâmica	*serrameeca*

east	este	*esht*
easy	fácil	*farseel*
eat	comer	*comair*
eczema	eczema	*eczma*
eel	enguia	*aingueeah*
egg	ovo	*ohvoo*
elastic band	elástico	*elashteecoo*
electric	eléctrico	*eletreecoo*
electricity	electricidade	*eletreesidard*
embassy	embaixada	*embysharda*
emergency brake	alarme	*alarm*
emergency exit	saída de emergência	*syeeda duh emairjensia*
emergency number	número de alarme	*noomeroo duh alarm*
emergency phone	telefone de emergência	*telefon duh emairjensia*
emergency triangle	triângulo de emergência	*treeangooloo duh emairjensia*
emery board	lima de unhas	*leema duh oonyash*
empty	vazio	*vazeeoo*
engaged	ocupado	*ocupardoo*
England	Inglaterra	*eenglaterra*
English, Englishman	inglês	*eenglayj*
enjoy	ter prazer	*tair prezzair*
entertainment (show) event	espectáculo	*espetarcooloo*
entertainment guide	revista de espectáculos	*reveeshta duh espetarcooloosh*
envelope	envelope	*envellop*
escort	acompanhante	*acompanyant*
evening (before 6pm)	tarde	*tard*
evening wear	traje de noite	*trarge duh noyt*
everything	tudo	*toodoo*
everywhere	por toda a parte	*por toeda ah part*
examine	examinar	*eezameenar*
excavations	escavações	*eshcavasoynsh*
excellent	óptimo	*otteemoo*
exchange	trocar	*troocar*
exchange rate	câmbio	*cambyoo*
excursion	excursão	*eshcoorsow*
exhibition	exposição	*eshpozisow*
exit	saida	*syeeda*
expenses	despesas	*deshpayzash*
expensive	caro	*caroo*
explain	explicar	*eeshpleecar*
express	comboio rápido	*comboyoo rapeedoo*
external	externo	*eeshtairnoo*
eye	olho	*olyoo*
eyedrops	gotas para os olhos	*gotash parra ooz olyoosh*
eyeshadow	sombra	*sombra*
eye specialist	oftalmologista	*oftalmolojeeshta*
eyeliner	lápis para os olhos	*larpeesh parra ooz olyoosh*

F

face	cara	*cara*
factory	fábrica	*fabreeca*
fair	feira	*fayra*

fall	cair	kyeer
family	família	fameelia
famous	famoso	famozoo
far away	longe	lonj
farm	quinta	keenta
farmer	agricultor	agreecooltor
farmer's wife	mulher do agricultor	moolyair do agreecooltor
fashion	moda	mohda
fast	rápido	rapeedoo
father	pai	pie
fault	culpa	coolpa
fax, send a	enviar um fax	enveear oom fax
February	fevereiro	fevverayroo
feel	sentir	senteer
feel like	ter vontade	tair vontard
fence	vedação	veddasow
ferry	barco	barcoo
fever	febre	febre
fill a tooth	obturar um dente	obtoorar oom dent
fill out	preencher	pree-enshair
filling	obturação	obtoorasow
film	rolo fotográfico	rolloo fotoograrfeecoo
film	filme	feelm
filter	filtro	feeltroo
find	achar	ashar
fine	multa	moolta
finger	dedo	daydoo
fire	fogueira	foogayra
fire	incêndio	eensendyoo
fire brigade	bombeiros	bombayroosh
fire escape	escada de	eshcarda duh
	emergência	emmairjensia
fire extinguisher	extintor	eshteentor
first	primeiro	preemayroo
first aid	primeiros socorros	preemayroosh socorroosh
first class	primeira classe	preemayra class
fish, to	pescar	peshcar
fish	peixe	paysh
fishing rod	cana de pesca	carna duh peshca
fit	assentar	assentar
fitness centre	centro de	sentroo duh
	manutenção física	manootensow feeseeca
fitness training	treino de	traynoo duh
	manutenção física	manootensow feeseeca
fitting room	gabinete de prova	gabeenet duh provva
fix/stick	colar/consertar	coollar/consairtar
flag	bandeira	bandayra
flash bulb	lâmpada do flash	lamparda doo flash
flash cube	flash em cubo	flash aim cooboo
flea market	feira da ladra	fayra da ladra
flight	vôo	voe
flight number	número do vôo	noomeroo duh voe
flood	inundação	eenoondasow
floor (building)	andar	andar
flour	farinha	fareenya
flyover	viaduto	veeadootoo
fly (insect)	mosca	moshca

Word list

15

123

fly (verb)	voar	*vooar*
fog	nevoeiro	*nevooayroo*
folding caravan	atrelado	*atrelardoo*
folkloric	folclórico	*folclorreecoo*
follow	seguir	*segear*
food	alimento	*allymentoo*
food poisoning	intoxicação alimentar	*eentoxeecasow allimentar*
foot	pé	*peh*
for	para	*parra*
for hire	aluga-se	*alooga-suh*
forbidden	proibido	*prooeebeedoo*
forehead	testa	*teshta*
foreign	estrangeiro	*eshtranjayroo*
forget	esquecer	*eshkessair*
fork	garfo	*garfoo*
form	impresso	*eempressoo*
fort	fortaleza	*fortalayza*
forward, send	enviar	*ainveeyar*
fountain	fonte	*font*
frame	armação	*armasow*
frank	franco	*francoo*
free	livre	*leevre*
free	gratuito	*gratooeetoo*
free time	tempo livre	*tempoo leevre*
freeze	congelar	*conjelar*
French	francês	*fransayj*
fresh	fresco	*freshcoo*
Friday	sexta-feira	*seshta fayra*
fried	frito	*freetoo*
fried egg	ovo estrelado	*ovoo shtrelardoo*
friend	amigo	*ameegoo*
friendly	simpático	*seemparteecoo*
friendly	amigavel	*ameegarvel*
fright	medo	*maydoo*
fringe	franja	*franja*
fruit	fruta	*froota*
fruit juice	sumo de frutas	*soomoo duh frootash*
frying pan	frigideira	*freejeedayra*
full	cheio	*shayoo*
fun	divertimento	*deevairteementoo*

G

gallery	galeria	*gallereea*
game	jogo	*jogoo*
garage	garagem	*gararjaim*
garden	jardim	*jardeem*
gastroenteritis	gastrenterite	*gashtrentaireet*
gauze	gaze	*gaz*
gear	velocidade	*velossidard*
gel	gel	*jel*
German	alemão	*allaymow*
get married	casar-se	*cazar-suh*
get off (e.g. a bus)	sair	*syeer*
gift	presente	*present*
gilt	dourado	*doorardoo*
ginger	gengibre	*jenjeebre*
girl	rapariga	*rapareega*

girlfriend	amiga	*ameega*
giro cheque	cheque dos correios	*sheck doosh coorayoosh*
giro guarantee card	cartão dos correios	*cartow doosj coorayoosh*
glass (for drinking)	copo	*copoo*
glass (window)	vidro	*veedroo*
glasses (sun-)	óculos (de sol)	*ocooloosh (duh sol)*
glide	planar	*plannar*
glove	luva	*loova*
glue	cola	*colla*
gnat	mosquito	*moshkeetoo*
go	ir	*ear*
go back	regressar	*regressar*
go out	sair	*syeer*
goat's cheese	queijo de cabra	*cayjoo duh cabra*
gold	ouro	*oroo*
golf course	campo de golfe	*campoo duh golf*
gone	perdido	*pairdeedoo*
good afternoon	boa tarde	*boa tard*
good evening	boa noite	*boa noyt*
good morning	bom dia	*bom deeah*
good night	boa noite	*boa noyt*
goodbye	adeus	*adayoosh*
goodbye	despedida	*deshpedeeda*
gram	grama	*grarma*
grams	gramas	*grarmash*
grandchild	neto/neta	*netoo/neta*
grandfather	avô	*avoe*
grandmother	avó	*avoh*
grape juice	sumo de uva	*soomoo di oova*
grapefruit	toranja	*tooranja*
grapes	uvas	*oovash*
grave	sepultura	*sepooltoora*
grease	gordura	*gordoora*
green	verde	*vaird*
green card	cartão verde	*cartow vaird*
greet	cumprimentar	*coompreementar*
grey haired	grisalho	*grizalyoo*
grill	grelhar	*grelyar*
grilled	grelhado	*grelyardoo*
grocer's shop	mercearia	*mercyareeah*
groceries	artigos de mercearia	*arteegoosh duh maircyareeah*
ground	chão	*shau*
ground beef	carne picada	*carn peecarda*
group	grupo	*groopoo*
guest house	pensão	*pensow*
guide (person, book)	guía	*gueeah*
guided tour	viagem guiada	*veearjaim gueearda*
gynaecologist	ginecologista	*jeenaycolojeeshta*

H

hair	cabelo	*cabayloo*
hairbrush	escova de cabelo	*eshcova duh cabayloo*
hairdresser	cabeleireiro, barbeiro	*cabelayrayroo, barbayroo*
hairpins	ganchos de cabelo	*ganshoosh duh cabayloo*
hairspray	laca para o cabelo	*laca parra oo cabayloo*
hairstyle	penteado	*pentyardoo*

half	meio	*mayoo*
half	metade	*metard*
half full	meio cheio	*mayoo shayoo*
hammer	martelo	*martelloo*
hand	mão	*mau*
handbrake	travão de mão	*travow duh mau*
handbag	mala	*mala*
handicrafts	artesanato	*artesanartoo*
handkerchief	lenço	*lensoo*
handmade	feito à mão	*faytoo ah mau*
happy	alegre	*allegre*
harbour	porto	*portoo*
hard	duro	*dooroo*
hat	chapéu	*shapayoo*
have dinner	jantar	*jantar*
hayfever	febre do feno	*febre doo fennoo*
hazelnut	avelã	*avelar*
head	cabeça	*cabaysa*
headache	dor de cabeça	*door duh cabaysa*
health	saúde	*sow-ood*
health food shop	loja de artigos	*loja duh arteegoosh*
	dietéticos	*dee-eteteecoosh*
hear	perceber	*pairsebbair*
hearing aid	aparelho auditivo	*aparellyoo owdeeteevoo*
heart	coração	*coorasow*
heart patient	cardíaco	*cardeeacoo*
heater	aquecimento	*akessimentoo*
heavy	pesado	*pezardoo*
heel	calcanhar	*calcanyar*
heel (shoe)	salto	*saltoo*
hello	óla	*ohla*
hello	viva	*veeva*
helmet	capacete	*cappaset*
help	ajudar	*ajoodar*
help	ajuda	*ajooda*
helping	dose	*doz*
herbal tea	chá de ervas	*shar di airvash*
herbs	ervas	*airvash*
here	aqui	*akee*
here you have	aqui tem	*akee taim*
herring	arenque	*arenk*
high	alto	*altoo*
high tide	maré cheia	*maray shaya*
highchair	cadeira de bebé	*cadayra duh baybay*
hiking	andar a pé	*andar ah peh*
hiking trip	excursão	*eshcoorsow ah peh*
hip	anca	*anca*
hire	alugar	*aloogar*
hitchhike	pedir boleia	*pedeer bolaya*
hobby	hobby	*obby*
holdup	assalto	*assaltoo*
holiday	feriado	*ferriardoo*
holiday	férias	*ferryash*
holiday house	casa de férias	*carza duh ferriash*
holiday village	aldeamento turístico	*aldayamentoo tooreeshteecoo*
homesickness	saudades	*sowdardesh*

honest	honesto	*hooneshtoo*
honey	mel	*mel*
horizontal	horizontal	*oreezontarl*
horrible	horroroso	*ororohzoo*
horse	cavalo	*cavarloo*
hospital	hospital	*oshpeetarl*
hospitality	hospitalidade	*oshpeetalidad*
hot	quente	*kent*
hotwater bottle	botija	*booteeja*
hot	picante	*peecant*
hotel	hotel	*ottel*
hour	hora	*oara*
house	casa	*carza*
household items	artigos domésticos	*arteegoosh doomeshteecoosh*
houses of parliament	edifício parlamentar	*edeefeesyoo parlamentar*
housewife	dona de casa	*donna duh carza*
how far?	a que distância?	*ah kay deeshtancia*
how long?	quanto tempo?	*cuarntoo tempoo?*
how much?	quanto?	*cuarntoo?*
how?	como?	*cohmoo?*
hurricane	ciclone	*seeeclon*
hurry	pressa	*pressa*
husband	marido	*mareedoo*
hut	cabana	*cabarna*
hyperventilation	hiperventilação	*eepairventeelasow*

I

ice cubes	cubos de gelo	*cooboosh duh jayloo*
icecream	gelado	*jelardoo*
idea	ideia	*eedaya*
identification	documento de identificação	*docoomentoo duh identeefeecasow*
identify	identificar	*eedenteefeecar*
ignition key	chave de contacto	*sharv duh contactoo*
ill	doente	*dooent*
illness	doença	*dooensa*
imagine	imaginar	*eemajeenar*
immediately	imediatamente	*eemediatament*
import duty	direito de importação	*deeraytoo di eemportasow*
impossible	impossível	*eempoosseevel*
impressions	impressões	*eempressoynsh*
in	dentro	*dentroo*
in the evening	à noitinha	*ah noyteenya*
in the morning	de manhã	*duh manyar*
included	incluído	*eenclooydoo*
included	inclusivo	*eenclooseevoo*
indicate	apontar	*appontar*
indicator	placa de sinalização	*placa duh seenaleezasow*
inexpensive	barato	*barartoo*
infection (viral/ bacterial)	infecção (virótica/ bacteriana)	*eenfecksow (veeroteeca/ bacteriana)*
inflammation	inflamação	*eenflammasow*
influenza	gripe	*greep*
information	informação	*eenformasow*

127

information	dados	dardoosh
information desk	balcão de informações	balcow di eenformasoynsh
injection	injecção	eenjecksow
injured	ferido	ferreedoo
inner tube	câmara de ar	cammara di ar
innocent	inocente	eenoocent
insect	insecto	eensectoo
insect bite	picadela de insecto	peecadella di eensectoo
insect repellant	repellente contra mosquitos	repellent contra moshkeetoosh
inside	dentro	dentroo
insole	palmilha	palmeelya
instructions	instruções	eenshtroosoynsh
insurance	seguro	segooroo
intermission	intervalo	eentervarloo
international	internacional	eentairnacionarl
interpreter	intérprete	eentairpret
intersection	cruzamento	croozamentoo
introduce oneself	apresentar-se	aprezentar-suh
invite	convidar	conveedar
iodine	iodo	yod
Ireland	Irlanda	earlanda
iron	ferro	fehroo
iron, to	passar a ferro	passar ah ferroo
iron	ferro de passar	ferroo duh passar
ironing board	tábua de passar	tabooah duh passar
island	ilha	eelya
Italian	italiano	eetaliarnoo
itch	comichão	comeechow

J

jack, monkey	macaco	makarkoo
jacket	casaco curto	cazarcoo coortoo
jam	doce	dose
January	janeiro	janayroo
jaw	maxilar	maksilar
jellyfish	alforreca	alfoorecka
jeweller	joalharia	jooalyareeah
jewellery	jóias	joyash
jog	fazer jogging	fazzair joggeeng
joke	piada	peearda
juice	sumo	soomoo
July	julho	joolyoo
jump leads	cabos para ligar a bateria	carboosh parra leegar a batereeah
jumper	camisola	cameezola
June	junho	joonyoo

K

key	chave	sharv
kilo	quilo	keeloo
kilometre	quilómetro	keelometroo
king	rei	ray
kiosk	quiosque	keeoshk
kiss (verb)	beijar	bayjar
kiss	beijo	bayjoo

kitchen	cozinha	_coozeenya_
knee	joelho	_jooelyoo_
knee socks	meias até o joelho	_mayash atay ow jooelyoo_
knife	faca	_facca_
knit	tricotar	_treecootar_
know	saber	_sabair_

L

lace	renda	_renda_
lace (shoe)	atacador	_attackadoor_
ladies'	lavabos de senhoras	_lavarboosh duh senyorash_
lake	lago	_largoo_
lamp	lâmpada	_lamparda_
land	terra	_terra_
lane	faixa de rodagem	_fysha duh roodarjaim_
language	língua	_leengwa_
large	grande	_grand_
last (previous)	anterior	_anterrior_
last	último	_oolteemoo_
last night	ontem à noite	_ontaim ah noyt_
late	tarde	_tard_
later, already	já	_jah_
laugh	rir	_rear_
launderette	lavandaria	_lavandareeah_
law	direito	_diraytoo_
laxative	purgativo	_poorgateevoo_
leak	furo	_fooroo_
leather	pele/couro	_pel/cooroo_
leather goods	artigos de pele	_arteegoosh duh pel_
leave	partir	_parteer_
leek	alho francês	_alyoo fransayj_
left	esquerda	_eshcairda_
left	à esquerda	_ah eshcairda_
left luggage	depósito de bagagem	_depozzeetoo duh bagarjaim_
leg	perna	_pairna_
lemon	limão	_leemow_
lend	emprestar	_aimpreshtar_
lens	lente	_lent_
lentils	lentilhas	_lenteelyash_
less	menos	_menoosh_
lesson	lição	_leesow_
letter	carta	_carta_
lettuce	alface	_alfass_
level crossing	passagem de nível	_passarjaim duh neevel_
library	biblioteca	_beebleeootehca_
lie	mentir	_menteer_
lie	deitarse	_daytarse_
lift (hitchhike)	boleia	_boolaya_
lift (in building)	elevador	_eelevadoor_
light (not dark)	claro	_claroo_
light (not heavy)	leve	_lev_
light	luz	_loosh_
light, to	acender	_assendair_
lighter	isqueiro	_eeshkayroo_
lighthouse	farol	_farol_
lightning	raio	_ryoo_

like	gostar de	*goshtar duh*
line	linha	*leenya*
linen	linho	*leenyoo*
lipstick	batôn	*baton*
liqueur	licor	*leecor*
liquorice	alcaçuz	*alcasooj*
listen	ouvir	*ohveer*
literature	literatura	*leeteratoora*
litre	litro	*leetroo*
little	pouco	*pohcoo*
live	morar	*moorar*
live together	viver junto	*veevair joontoo*
lobster	lagosta	*lagoshta*
local	local	*loocal*
lock	fechadura	*feshadoora*
long	comprido	*compreedoo*
long lasting	de longa duração	*duh longa doorasow*
look	olhar	*oolyar*
look for	procurar	*procoorar*
lorry	camião	*cammyow*
lose	perder	*pairdair*
loss	perda	*pairda*
lost	perdido	*pairdeedoo*
lost property office	achados e perdidos	*ashardoosh ee perdeedooz*
lotion	loção	*loosow*
loud	alto	*altoo*
love, to	gostar/amar	*goshtar/amar*
love	amor	*amor*
low	baixo	*byshoo*
low tide	maré baixa	*maray bysha*
luck	sorte	*sort*
luggage	bagagem	*bagarjaim*
luggage locker	cofre de bagagem	*cofre duh bagarjaim*
lunch	almoço	*almoesoo*
lungs	pulmões	*poolmoynsh*

M

macaroni	macarrão	*macarrow*
machine (vending)	vendedor automático	*vendador owtoomateecoo*
madam	senhora	*senyora*
magazine	revista	*reveeshta*
mail	correio	*coorayoo*
main post office	correio central	*coorayoo centrarl*
main road	estrada	*eshtrarda*
make an appointment	marcar um encontro	*marcar oom aincontroo*
make love	fazer amor	*fazzair amor*
makeshift	provisório	*prooveesoryoo*
man	homem	*omaim*
manager	gerente	*jerrent*
mandarin	tangerina	*tanjereena*
manicure	manicure	*manicure*
map	mapa	*mapa*
marble	mármore	*marmora*
March	março	*marsoo*

margarine	margarina	margareena
marina	marina	mareena
market	mercado	mercardoo
marriage, wedding	casamento	cazamento
married	casado	cazardoo
mass	missa	meessa
massage	massagem	massarjaim
matt	sem brilho	saim breelyoo
match	desafio/jogo	dezafyoo/jogoo
matches	fósforos	foshforoosh
May	maio	myoo
maybe	talvez	talvayj
mayonnaise	maionese	myonez
mayor	presidente da	prezeedent da
	câmara/prefeito	cammara/preffaytoo
meal	refeição	refaysow
mean	significar	seegneefeecar
meat	carne	carn
medication,	medicamento/	medicamentoo/
medicine	remédio	remedyoo
meet	conhecer	coonyessair
melon	melão	melow
membership	adesão	adezow
menstruate	menstruar	menshtrooar
menstruation	menstruação	menshtruasow
menu	menu, ementa	menoo, ementa
menu of the day	menu do dia	menoo doo dia
message	mensagem	mensarjaim
metal	metal	mettal
meter	taxímetro	tackseemetroo
metre	metro	metroo
migraine	enxaqueca	ainshakeka
milk	leite	layt
millimetre	milímetro	meeleemetroo
milometer	contaquilómetros	conta keelometroosh
mineral water	água mineral	agwa meeneral
minute	minuto	meenootoo
mirror	espelho	shpelyoo
miss	sentir a falta	senteer ah falta
missing person	desaparecido	dezaparesseedoo
mistake	erro	ehroo
mistake	engano	aingarnoo
misunderstanding	malentendido	mal entendeedoo
mixture	mistura	meeshtoora
modern art	arte moderna	art mooderna
molar	molar	moolar
moment	um momento	oom momentoo
monastery	mosteiro	mooshtayroo
Monday	segunda-feira	segoonda fayra
money	dinheiro	deenyayroo
month	mês	mayj
moped	bicicleta motorizada	beeceecletta
		mottooreezarda
more and more	cada vez mais	cadda vaij mysh
morning-after pill	pílula `morning after'	peeloola `morning-after'
mosque	mesquita	meshkeeta
motel	motel	mohtel

mother	mãe	my
motor cross	motociclismo	motooseecleejmoo
motorbike	motocicleta	motooseeclayta
motorboat	barco a motor	barcoo ah motor
motorway	autoestrada	owtooshtrarda
mountain	monte	mont
mountain hut	refúgio	refoogyoo
mountaineering	alpinismo	alpeeneejmoo
mountaineering shoes	sapatos de alpinismo	sapartoosh duh alpeeneejmoo
mouse	rato	rartoo
mouth	boca	boca
much/many	muito/muitos	mweentoo/mweentoosh
multistorey car park	parque de vários andares	park duh varyooz andaresh
muscle	músculo	mooshcooloo
muscle spasms	cãibras	kybraj
museum	museu	moosayoo
mushrooms	cogumelos	cogoomeloosh
music	música	mooseeca
musical	musical	mooseecal
mussels	mexilhões	mesheelyoynsh
mustard	mostarda	mooshtarda

N

nail	unha	oonya
nail (metal)	prego	praygoo
nail polish	verniz para as unhas	verneej parra az oonyash
nail polish remover	acetona para as unhas	assaytona parra az oonyash
nail scissors	tesoura de unhas	tezora di oonyash
naked	nu	noo
nappy	fralda	fralda
nationality	nacionalidade	nasionaleedad
natural	naturalmente	natooralment
nature	natureza	natoorayza
naturism	naturismo	natooreejmoo
naturist beach	praia de naturistas	prya duh natooreeshtash
nauseous	enjoativo	ainjooateevoo
near	perto de	pairtoo duh
nearby	perto	pairtoo
necessary	necessário	necessaryoo
neck	pescoço	peshcossoo
necklace	fio	feeoo
nectarine	nectarina	nectareena
needle	agulha	agoolya
negative	negativo	negateevoo
neighbours	vizinhos	veezeenyoosh
nephew	sobrinho	soobreenyoo
never	nunca	noonca
new	novo	nohvoo
news	notícias	nooteeciash
newspaper	jornal	jornal
next	seguinte	segeent
next to	ao lado	ow lardoo
nice (friendly)	simpático	seemparteecoo
nice (to taste)	agradável, bonito	agradarvel, booneetoo

niece	sobrinha	soobreenya
night	noite	noyt
night duty	serviço nocturno	sairveesoo noctoornoo
nightclub	clube nocturno	cloob noctoornoo
nightlife	vida nocturna	veeda noctoorna
no one	ninguém	neengaim
no	não	now
no overtaking	proibido de ultrapassar	prooeebeedoo duh ooltrapassar
noise	barulho	baroolyoo
nonstop	directo (sem paragens)	deerectoo (saim pararjainsh)
normal	normal	normal
north	norte	nort
nose	nariz	nareej
nose drops	gotas para o nariz	gotash parra oo nareej
notepaper	papel de escrever	papel duh eshcrevair
nothing	nada	narda
November	novembro	noovembroo
nowhere	em parte nenhuma	aim part nenyooma
number	número	noomeroo
number plate	matrícula	matreecoola
nurse	enfermeira	ainfairmayra
nutmeg	noz moscada	noj mooshcarda
nuts (mixed)	nozes (mistura)	nozesh (meeshtoora)

O

October	outubro	ohtoobroo
offer	oferecer	ofressair
office	escritório	eshcreetoryoo
oil	óleo	ollyoo
oil level	nível do óleo	neevel doo ollyoo
ointment	pomada	poomarda
ointment for burns	pomada contra queimaduras	poomarda contra kaymadurash
okay	de acordo	di acordoo
old	velho	velyoo
olive oil	azeite	azayt
olives	azeitonas	azaytonash
omelette	omeleta	omelayta
on	em cima de	aim seema duh
on board	a bordo	ah bordoo
on the right	direito	diraytoo
on the way	no caminho	noo cameenyoo
oncoming car	em sentido contrário	aim senteedoo contraryoo
oneway traffic	trânsito de sentido único	transeetoo duh senteedoo ooneecoo
onion	cebola	sebolla
open	aberto	abairtoo
open	abrir	abreer
opera	ópera	opera
operate	operar	operar
operator (telephone)	telefonista	telefoneeshta
operetta	opereta	opereta
opposite	em frente	aim frent
optician	oculista	occooleeshta
orange (colour)	cor de laranja	coor duh laranja

orange	laranja	*laranja*
orange juice	sumo de laranja	*soomoo duh laranja*
order (in -,) tidy	em ordem	*aim ordaim*
order	encomenda	*aincoomenda*
order, to	encomendar	*aincoomendar*
other	outro	*ohtroo*
other side	do outro lado	*doo ohtroo lardoo*
outside	fora	*forra*
overtake	ultrapassar	*ooltrapassar*
oysters	ostras	*oshtrash*

P

packed lunch	merenda/lanche	*merenda/lansh*
packet (of cigarettes)	pacote (de cigarros)	*packot (duh seegarroosh)*
page	página	*parjeena*
pain	dor	*door*
painkiller	analgésico	*analjezeecoo*
paint	tinta	*teenta*
painting	pintura	*peentoora*
palace	palácio	*palassio*
pan	panela	*panella*
pancake	crepe	*crep*
pane	vidro	*veedroo*
pants, briefs, knickers	cuecas	*cooeckash*
panty liner	penso de protecção	*pensoo duh prootecsow*
paper	papel	*papel*
paprika	pimento	*peementoo*
paraffin oil	petróleo	*petrollyoo*
parasol	chapéu de sol	*shapayoo duh sol*
parcel	encomenda postal	*aimcoomenda pooshtal*
parcel	pacote	*packot*
pardon	desculpe	*deshcoolp*
parents	pais	*pysh*
park	parque	*park*
park	estacionar	*estassionar*
parking space	lugar para estacionar	*loogar parra eshtassionar*
parsley	salsa	*salsa*
part (car)	peça	*pessa*
partition	separação	*separação*
partner	companheiro	*companyayroo*
party	festa	*feshta*
passable (road)	transitável	*transeetarvel*
passenger	passageiro	*passajayroo*
passport	passaporte	*passaport*
passport photo	foto tipo passe	*fotoo teepoo pass*
patient	doente	*dooent*
pavement	passeio/calçada	*passayoo/calsarda*
pay	pagar	*paggar*
pay the bill	pagar a conta	*pagar a conta*
peach	pêssego	*pessaygoo*
peanuts	amendoins	*amendooeensh*
pear	pera	*paira*
peas	ervilhas	*airveelyash*
pedal	pedalo	*pedarloo*
pedestrian crossing	passagem para peões	*passarjaim parra peeoynsh*

English	Portuguese	Pronunciation
pedicure	pedicure	pedicure
pen	caneta	canetta
pencil (hard/soft)	lápis (duro/macio)	larpeej (dooroo/maseeyoo)
penis	pénis	penneej
penknife	canivete	canivet
pepper	pimenta	peementa
performance (show)	representação	representasow
perfume	perfume	perfoom
perm	permanente	permanent
perm, to have a...	fazer uma permanente	fazzair ooma permanent
permit	licença	leesensa
person	pessoa	pessoa
personal	pessoal	pessoal
petrol	gasolina	gazooleena
petrol station	estação de serviço/ posto de gasolina	eshtasow duh serveesoo/ poshtoo duh gazooleena
pets	animais de estimação	animysh duh eshteemasow
pharmacy	farmácia	farmassia
phone (tele-)	telefone	telefon
phone (verb)	telefonar	telefoonar
phone box	cabine telefónica	cabeen telefoneeca
phone directory	lista telefónica	leeshta telefoneeca
phone number	número de telefone	noomeroo duh telefon
photo	fotografia	fotografeea
photocopier	máquina copiadora	markeena copiadoora
photocopy (verb)	fotocopiar	fotoocoopiar
photocopy	fotocópia	fotoocopia
pick up	ir buscar	ear booshcar
picnic	piquenique	peekneek
piece of clothing	peça de roupa	pessa duh roepa
pier	pontão/cais	pontow/kysh
pigeon	pombo	pomboo
pill (contraceptive)	pílula anticoncepcional	peeloola anticonsepcional
pillow	almofada	almoofarda
pillowcase	fronha	fronya
pin	alfinete	alfeenet
pineapple	ananás	ananash
pipe	cachimbo	casheemboo
pipe tobacco	tabaco para cachimbo	tabacoo parra casheemboo
pity	(ter) pena	(tair) penna
place of interest	lugares turísticos	loogaresh tooreeshteecoosh
plan	planta	planta
plant	planta	planta
plasters	pensos	pensoosh
plastic	plástico	plashteecoo
plate, dish, course	prato	prartoo
platform	linha	leenya
platform	cais	kysh
play, (theatre)	peça de teatro	pessa duh teeartroo
play	brincar	breencar
play basketball	jogar basquetebol	joogar bashketboll

play draughts	jogar às damas	joogar as damash
play golf	jogar golfe	joogar golf
play tennis	jogar ténis	joogar teneej
playground	jardim infantil	jardeem eenfanteel
playing cards	cartas de jogar	cartash duh joogar
pleasant	agradável	agradarvel
please	se faz favor	suh faj favvor
pleasure	prazer	prazzair
plum	ameixa	amaysha
point	indicar	eendeecar
poison	veneno	venenoo
police	polícia	poleesia
police station	posto da polícia	poshtoo da poleesia
police officer	polícia	poleesia
pond	tanque	tank
pony	pónei	pohnay
pop concert	concerto de pop	consairtoo duh pop
population	população	poopoolasow
pork	carne de porco	carn duh porcoo
port-wine	vinho do Porto	veenyoo doo portoo
porter	bagageiro	bagajayroo
porter	porteiro	portayroo
post code	código postal	codeegoo pooshtal
post office	agência do correio	ajencia do coorayoo
postage	porte	port
postbox	caixa de correio	kysha duh coorayoo
postcard	postal	pooshtal
postman	carteiro	cartayroo
potato	batata	batarta
poultry	aves	arvesh
pound	libra	leebra
powdered milk	leite em pó	layt aim poh
power point	ligação eléctrica/	leegasow eeletreeca/
	tomada	toomarda
pram	carrinho de bébé	carreenyoo duh baybay
prawns	camarões	cammaroynsh
precious	precioso	pressiozoo
prefer, to	preferir	prefereer
preference	preferência	preferensia
pregnant	grávida	graveeda
present	presente	prezzent
pressure	stress	shtress
price	preço	praysoo
price list	lista de preços	leeshta duh praysoosh
print	imprimir	eempreemeer
print (verb)	fazer cópias	fazair coppyash
print	cópia	cohpya
probably	provavelmente	proovarvelment
problem	problema	prooblayma
profession	profissão	proofeesow
programme	programa	proograma
pronounce	pronunciar	proonunciar
propane/butane	gás de campismo	gaj duh campeejmoo
(camping gas)	(propano/butano)	(proparnoo/bootarnoo)
provident fund	caixa de previdência	kysha duh preveedencia
prune	ameixa seca	amaysha seca
pudding	pudim	poodeem

pull (tooth)	tirar (dente)	*teerar (dent)*
pull a muscle	distender um músculo	*deeshtendair oom mooshcooloo*
pure	puro	*pooroo*
purple	violeta	*veeooleta*
purse	portamoedas	*porta mooaydash*
push	empurrar	*aimpurrar*
puzzle	puzzle	*puzzel*
pyjamas	pijama	*peejama*

Q

quarter	quarto	*cwartoo*
quarter of an hour	quarto de hora	*cwartoo duh ora*
queen	rainha	*ryeenya*
question	pergunta	*pairgoonta*
quick	rápido	*rapeedoo*
quiet	calmo	*calmoo*

R

radio	rádio	*rardyoo*
railways	caminhos de ferro	*cameenyoosh duh feroo*
rain	chuva	*shoova*
rain, to	chover	*choovair*
raincoat	impermeável	*eempairmeearvel*
raisins	passas	*passash*
rape	violação	*veeolasow*
rapids	cachoeiro	*cashooayroo*
raspberries	framboesas	*frambooayzash*
raw	cru	*croo*
raw vegetables	legumes crus	*legoomesh croosh*
razor blades	giletes	*geeletsch*
read	ler	*lair*
ready	pronto	*prontoo*
receipt	talão, recibo	*tallow, resseeboo*
recipe	receita	*resayta*
reclining chair	cadeira-cama	*cadayra camma*
recommend	recomendar	*recoomendar*
rectangle	rectângulo	*retangooloo*
red	encarnado/vermelho	*encarnardoo/vermelyoo*
red wine	vinho tinto	*veenyoo teentoo*
reduction	desconto	*deshcontoo*
refrigerator	frigorífico	*freegoreefeecoo*
regards	cumprimentos	*coompreementoosh*
region	região	*rejiow*
registered	registado	*rejeeshtardo*
registration document	livrete	*leevret*
relatives	família	*fameelia*
reliable	confiável	*confeearvel*
religion	religião	*releegeeow*
rent out	alugar	*aloogar*
repair	reparar/concertar	*reparar/consairtar*
repairs	reparações/consertos	*reparasoynsh/consairtoosh*
repeat	repetir	*repeteer*
report	relatório	*relatoryoo*
resent	levar a mal	*levar ah mal*

responsible	responsável	responsarvel
rest	descansar	deshcansar
restaurant	restaurante	reshtowrant
result	resultado	resooltardoo
retired	reformado	reformardoo
return (ticket)	ida e volta (bilhete)	eeda ee vollta (beelyet)
reverse (vehicle)	fazer marcha atrás	fazair marsha atraj
rheumatism	reumatismo	rayoomateesjmoo
rice	arroz	arroj
ridiculous	estúpido/ridículo	eshtoopeedoo/ reedeecooloo
riding (horseback)	andar a cavalo	andar ah cavarloo
riding school	picadeiro	peecadayroo
right	para a direita	parra ah dirayta
right of way	prioridade	preeorridard
ripe	maduro	madooroo
risk	risco	reeshcoo
river	rio	reeoo
road	rua	rooah
roadway	estrada	estrarda
roasted	assado	assardoo
rock	rocha	rosha
roll	pãozinho (sem manteiga)	powzeenyoo (saim mantayga)
rolling tobacco	cigarro de enrolar	seegarroo di ainroolar
roof rack	portabagagem	porta bagarjaim
room	quarto	cwartoo
room number	número do quarto	noomeroo doo cwartoo
room service	serviço de quarto	sairveesoo duh cwartoo
rope	cordel/corda	cordel/corda
rosé	rosé	rozay
roundabout	rotunda	rotoonda
route	caminho	cameenyoo
rowing boat	barco à remos	barcoo ah remoosh
rubber	borracha	borasha
rubbish	lixo	leeshoo
rubbish bag	saco do lixo	sarcoo duh leeshoo
rubbish, nonsense	estupidez	eshtoopeedej
rucksack	mochila	mosheela
rude	malcriado	malcreeardo
ruins	ruínas	roo-eenash
run into	encontrar	aincontrar

S

sad	triste	treesht
safari	safari	safaree
safe	seguro	segooroo
safe	cofre	cofre
safety pin	alfinete de segurança	alfeenet duh segooransa
sail	velejar	velejar
sailing boat	barco à vela	barcoo ah vella
salad	salada	salarda
salad oil	óleo para salada	ollyoo parra salarda
salami	salame	salam
sale	saldo/liquidação	saldoo/leekeedasow
salt	sal	sal

same	mesmo	*mejmoo*
sandy beach	praia de areia	*prya duh arraya*
sanitary pad	penso higiénico	*pensoo eegeneecoo*
sardines	sardinhas	*sardeenyash*
satisfied	satisfeito	*sateeshfaytoo*
Saturday	sábado	*sarbadoo*
sauce	molho	*molyoo*
sauna	sauna	*sowna*
sausage (preserved)	chouriço	*shooreesoo*
savoury	salgado	*salgardoo*
say	dizer	*deezair*
scarf	cachecol	*cashcol*
scenic walk	percurso turístico	*paircoorsoo tooreeshteecoo*
school	escola	*shcola*
scissors	tesoura	*tezora*
scooter	scooter	*scootair*
scorpion	escorpião	*eshcorpyow*
Scotland	Escócia	*eshcossia*
scrambled eggs	ovos mexidos	*ovoosh mesheedoosh*
screw	parafuso	*parrafoozoo*
screwdriver	chave de fenda	*sharv duh fenda*
sculpture	escultura	*eshcooltoora*
sea	mar	*mar*
seasick	enjoado	*ainjoooardoo*
seat	lugar sentado	*loogar sentardoo*
secondhand	segunda mão	*segoonda mau*
second	segundo	*segoondoo*
sedative	sedativo	*sedateevoo*
see, visit	visitar	*veezeetar*
send	enviar	*ainvyar*
sentence	frase	*fraz*
September	setembro	*setembroo*
serious, grave	grave	*grarv*
serious, responsible	sério	*sairyoo*
service	serviço	*serveesoo*
serviette	guardanapo	*gwardanarpoo*
sewing thread	linhas de costura	*leenyash duh coshtoora*
shade	sombra	*sombra*
shallow	pouco fundo	*pohcoo foondoo*
shammy	camurça	*camoorsa*
shampoo	champô	*shampoh*
shark	tubarão	*toobarow*
shave	barbear	*barbyar*
shaver	máquina de barbear	*markeena duh barbyar*
shaving brush	pincel de barba	*peensel duh barba*
shaving cream	creme de barbear	*crem duh barbyar*
shaving soap	sabão de barbear	*sabow duh barbyar*
sheet	lençol	*lensol*
sherry	xerez	*sherayj*
shirt	camisa	*cameeza*
shoe	sapato	*sapartoo*
shoe polish	pomada de engraixar	*poomarda di aingryshar*
shoe shop	sapataria	*sapattareeah*
shoemaker	sapateiro	*sappatayroo*
shop	loja	*loja*
shop assistant	empregada	*aimpregarda*

139

shop window	montra	*montra*
shopping	fazer compras	*fazzair comprash*
shopping centre	centro comercial	*sentroo coomerciarl*
short	curto	*coortoo*
short circuit	curtocircuito	*coortoo seercooeetoo*
shorts	calças curtas	*calsash coortash*
shoulder	ombro	*ombroo*
show	espectáculo	*eshpetarcooloo*
shower	duche	*doosh*
shutter (camera)	diafragma	*deeafragma*
sieve	peneira	*penayra*
sign	painel/sinal	*pynel/seenal*
sign	assinar	*asseenar*
signature	assinatura	*assenatoora*
silence	silêncio	*seelensyoo*
silver	prata	*prarta*
silverplated	prateado	*pratyardoo*
simple	simples	*seemplesh*
single	solteiro	*soltayroo*
single	individual	*eendeeveedual*
single ticket	bilhete de ida	*beelyet duh eeda*
sir	senhor	*senyor*
sister	irmã	*eermar*
sit	sentar-se	*sentar-suh*
size	número	*noomeroo*
size	tamanho	*tamanyoo*
skate	patinar	*pateenar*
skimmed	meio gordo	*mayoo gordoo*
skin	pele	*pel*
skirt	saia	*syah*
sleep	dormir	*doormeer*
sleeping car	carruagem cama	*carruarjaim camma*
sleeping pills	comprimidos para dormir	*compreemeedoosh parra doormeer*
slide	diapositivo	*deeapozeeteevoo*
slip road	entrada para a rodovia	*entrarda parra ah rodooveeah*
slow	devagar	*deevagar*
slow train	comboio ronceiro	*comboyoo ronsayroo*
small	pequeno	*peekenoo*
small change	dinheiro trocado, troco	*deenyayroo troocardoo, trocoo*
smell, to	cheirar mal	*shayrar mal*
smoke	fumo	*foomoo*
smoke	fumar	*foomar*
smoked	fumado	*foomardoo*
smoked dried ham, Parma style	presunto	*prezoontoo*
smoking compartment	carruagem para fumadores	*carruarjaim parra foomadoresh*
snake	serpente	*sairpent*
snorkel	máscara de mergulho	*mashcara duh mairgoolyoo*
soap	sabão	*sabow*
soap box	caixa de sabonete	*kysha duh saboonet*
soccer	futebol	*footbol*
soccer match	partida de futebol	*parteeda duh footbol*

socket	tomada	toomarda
socks	meias	mayash
soft drink	refresco/refrigerante	refreshcoo/refrijerant
sole (foot)	sola	solla
sole (fish)	linguado	leengwardoo
solicitor	advogado	advoogardoo
someone	alguém	algaim
sometimes	por vezes	por vayzesh
somewhere	em algum lugar	aim algoom loogar
son	filho	feelyoo
soon	já	jar
sorbet	sorvete	sorvet
sore/wound	ferida	fereeda
sore throat	dor de garganta	dor duh garganta
sorry	desculpe	deshcoolp
sort/type	espécie	eshpess
soup	sopa	soppa
sour	ácido	asseedoo
sour cream	natas azedas	nartash azaydash
source	fonte	font
south	sul	sool
souvenir	lembrança	lembransa
spaghetti	espaguete	shparget
spanner (open-ended)	chave de porcas	sharv duh porcash
spare	reserva	rezairva
spare parts	peças sobressalentes	pessash sobresalentesh
spare tyre	pneu sobressalente	pnayoo sobresalent
spare wheel	roda sobressalente	rodda sobresalent
speak	falar	falar
special	especial	eshpessiarl
specialist	especialista	eshpessialeeshta
specialty	especialidade	eshpessialidade
speed limit	velocidade máxima	velossidard masseema
spell	soletrar	sooletrar
spicy	picante	peecant
splinter	farpa	farpa
spoon, spoonful	colher	coolyair
sport	desporto	deshportoo
sports centre	centro de desportos	sentroo duh deshpoortoosh
spot (place)	lugar	loogar
sprain	torcer	torssair
spring	primavera	preemavayra
square	praça	prassa
square	quadrado	cuardrardoo
square metres	metro quadrado	metroo cuardrardoo
squash	jogar squash	joogar squash
stadium	estádio	shtardyoo
stain	nódoa	noddooah
stain remover	tiranódoas	teer noddooash
stairs	escada	eshcarda
stalls (theatre)	platéia	plataya
stamp	selo	selloo
start	começar	coomehsar
station	estação	eshtasow

statue	estátua	eshtartooah
stay (accommodation)	hospedar-se	oshpedar-se
stay (be)	ficar	feecar
stay	estadia	eshtadeeah
steal	roubar	roobar
steel	aço	ahsoo
stench	mau cheiro	mau shayroo
sting	picar	peecar
stitch (medical)	ponto	pontoo
stitch, to	coser	coozair
stockings	meias	mayash
stomach	estômago/barriga	eshtomagoo/bareega
stomach ache	dor de barriga/ estômago	door duh bareega/ eshtomagoo
stomach cramps	cólica	colleeca
stools	fezes	fayzesh
stop, to	parar	parrar
stop	paragem	pararjaim
stopover	escala	eshcala
storm	tempestade	tempashtard
straight	liso	leezoo
straight ahead	em frente	aim frent
straw	palhinha	palyeenya
strawberries	morangos	moorangoosh
street	rua	rooah
strike	greve	grev
strong	forte	fort
study	estudar	eshtoodar
stuffing	recheio	reshayoo
subscriber's number	número de telefone/ assinante	noomeroo duh telefon/asseenant
subtitled	legendado	lejendardoo
succeed	sair bem	syeer baim
sugar	açúcar	assoocar
sugar lumps	cubos de açúcar	cooboosh di assoocar
suit	fato	fartoo
suitcase	mala	mala
summer	verão	verow
summertime	horário de verão	oraryoo duh verow
sun	sol	sol
sun hat	chapéu de sol	shapayoo duh sol
sunbathe	tomar banho de sol	toomar banyoo duh sol
Sunday	domingo	doomeengoo
sunglasses	óculos de sol	ocooloosh duh sol
sunrise	nascer do sol	nashsair doo sol
sunset	pôr do sol	por doo sol
sunstroke	insolação	eensolasow
suntan lotion	creme solar	crem soolar
suntan oil	óleo solar	ollyoo soolar
supermarket	supermercado	supairmaircardoo
surcharge	suplemento	sooplementoo
surf	fazer surfe	fazzair surf
surf board	prancha de surfe	pransha duh surf
surgery	consultório	consooltoryoo
surname	apelido	apelleedoo
surprise	surpresa	soorprayza
swallow	engolir	aingooleer

swamp	pântano	pantarnoo
sweat	suor	soo-or
sweet (sugar)	rebuçado	reboosardoo
sweet (nice)	amoroso	amorozoo
sweet	doce	dose
sweetcorn	milho	meelyoo
sweeteners	adoçantes	adoosantesh
sweets	doces	dosesh
swim	nadar	nadar
swimming pool	piscina	peeshseena
swimming trunks	calções de banho	calsoynsh duh barnyoo
swindle	fraude	frowd
switch	interruptor	eenterruptor
synagogue	sinagoga	seenagoga

T

table	mesa	mayza
table tennis	ténis de mesa	teneej duh mayza
tablet	comprimido	compreemeedoo
take a photograph	tirar uma fotografia	teerar ooma fotografeeah
take	tomar	toomar
take, last	durar	durar
taken, engaged	ocupado	occoopardoo
talcum powder	(pó de) talco	(poh duh) talcoo
talk	falar	falar
tall	alto	altoo
tampons	tampões	tampoynsh
tanned	bronzeado	bronzyardoo
tap	torneira	tornayra
tap water	água da torneira	agwa da tornayra
taste	provar	proovar
taxi	táxi	tarksy
taxi rank	praça de táxis	prassa duh tarkseesh
tea	chá	shar
teapot	bule	bool
teaspoon	colher de chá	coolyair duh shar
telegram	telegrama	telegrarma
telephoto lens	teleobjectiva	tele objeteeva
television	televisão	televeesow
telex	telex	telex
temperature (weather)	temperatura	temperatoora
temporary filling	obturação temporária	obtoorasow temporaria
tender	tenro	tenroo
tennis ball	bola de ténis	bola duh teneej
tennis court	campo de ténis	campoo duh teneej
tennis racket	raquete de ténis	raket duh teneej
tenpin bowling	jogar bowling	joogar bowling
tent	tenda	tenda
tent peg	espia/estaca	eshpeea/eshtarca
terrace	esplanada	eshplanarda
terribly	terrivelment	terreevelment
thank	agradecer	agradaysair
thank you	muito obrigado	mweentoo obrigardoo
thanks	obrigado	obrigardoo
the day after tomorrow	depois de amanhã	depoysh di amanyar

theatre	teatro	teeartroo
theft	roubo	roeboo
there	ali	alee
thermal bath	banho termal	barnyoo termal
thermometer	termómetro	termometroo
thick	espesso	eshpessoo
thief	ladrão	ladrow
thigh	coxa	cosha
thin	fino	feenoo
thin	magro	magroo
things	coisas	coyzash
think	pensar	pensar
third	terço/terceiro	tairsoo/tairsayroo
thirsty, to be	ter (estar com) sede	tair (eshtar com) sed
this afternoon	esta tarde	eshta tard
this evening, tonight	esta noite	eshta noyt
this morning	esta manhã	eshta manyar
thread	fiozinho/linha	feeyoozeenyoo/leenya
throat	garganta	garganta
throat lozenges	pastilhas para a garganta	pashteelyash parra a garganta
thunderstorm	trovoada	troovooarda
Thursday	quinta-feira	keenta fayra
ticket	bilhete	beelyet
ticket window, bank counter	guiché	gueeshay
tickets	bilhetes	beelyetsch
tidy	arrumar	arroomar
tie	gravata	gravata
tights	collants	collan
time	tempo	tempoo
timer	timer	timer
timetable	horário	oraryoo
tin	lata	larta
tip	gorjeta	gorjeta
tissues	lenços de papel	lensoosh duh papel
toast (drink)	brinde	breend
toast (bread)	torrada/tosta	toorarda/toshta
tobacco	tabaco	tabarcoo
today	hoje	oarge
toe	dedo do pé	daydoo doo peh
together	juntos	joontoosh
toilet	lavabos	lavarboosh
toilet paper	papel higiénico	papel eegeneecoo
toiletries	artigos de toilete	arteegoosh duh twalet
tomato	tomate	toomat
tomato purée	puré de tomate	pooray duh toomat
tomato sauce	ketchup	keshoop
tomorrow	amanhã	amarnyar
tongue	língua	leengwa
tonic water	água tónica	agwa toneeca
too much	demais	demysh
tools	ferramenta	ferramenta
tooth	dente	dent
toothache	dor de dentes	door duh dentsh
toothbrush	escova de dentes	eshcova de dentsh
toothpaste	pasta de dentes	pashta duh dentsh

toothpick	palito	*paleetoo*
top up	encher	*ainshair*
total	total	*tootal*
tough	duro	*dooroo*
tour	passeio (turístico)	*passayoo (tooreeshteecoo)*
tour guide	guía turístico	*gueeah tooreeshteeco*
tourist class	classe turística	*class tooreeshteeca*
Tourist Information office	agência de turismo	*ajencia duh tooreejmoo*
tourist menu	ementa turística	*ementa tooreeshteeca*
tourist ticket	bilhete turístico	*beelyet tooreeshteeco*
tow, to	rebocar	*reboocar*
towel	toalha	*tooalya*
tower	torre	*torr*
towing cable	cabo para rebocar	*carboo parra reboocar*
town	cidade	*sidarde*
town hall	câmara municipal	*carmara mooneeceepal*
toys	brinquedo	*breenkaydoo*
traffic	trânsito	*transeetoo*
traffic light	semáforo	*semafforoo*
train	comboio	*comboyoo*
train ticket	bilhete de combóio	*beelyet duh comboyoo*
train timetable	horário de combóio	*oraryoo duh comboyoo*
trainers	ténis	*teneej*
translate	traduzir	*tradoozeer*
travel	viajar	*veeajar*
travel agent	agência de viagens	*ajencia duh veearjainsh*
travel guide	guia	*gueeah*
traveller	viajante	*veeajant*
traveller's cheque	traveller cheque	*traveller sheck*
treacle/syrup	xarope	*sharop*
treatment	tratamento	*tratamentoo*
triangle	triângulo	*treeangooloo*
trim (hair)	aparar	*apparrar*
trip	passeio	*passayoo*
trip	excursão	*eshcoorsow*
trip	viagem	*veearjaim*
trip	voltinha	*volteenya*
trouble	dor	*door*
trout	truta	*troota*
trunk call	chamada interurbana	*shamarda eenter oorbarna*
trustworthy person	pessoa de confiança	*pessoa duh confeeansa*
try on	provar	*proovar*
tube	bisnaga	*beejnarga*
Tuesday	terça-feira	*tairsa fayra*
tumble drier	máquina de secar	*markeena duh seccar*
tuna	atum	*atoom*
tunnel	túnel	*toonel*
turn	turno	*toornoo*
TV	TV	*tayvay*
TV guide	guia de TV	*gueeah duh tayvay*
tweezers	pinça	*peensa*
tyre	pneu	*pnayoo*
tyre lever	desmontador	*dejmontador*
tyre pressure	pressão dos pneus	*pressow doosh penayoosh*

U

ugly	feio	*fayoo*
umbrella	chapéu de chuva	*shapayoo duh shoova*
under	em baixo	*aim byshoo*
underground	metropolitano	*metroopooleetarnoo*
underground railway system	rede de metropolitano	*red duh metroopooleetarnoo*
underground station	estação de metropolitano	*eshtasow duh metroopooleetarnoo*
understand	compreender	*compree-endair*
underwear	roupa interior	*roepa eenterrior*
undress	despir	*despeer*
unemployed	desempregado	*dezaimpregardoo*
uneven	acidentado	*assdentardoo*
university	universidade	*ooniversidarde*
unleaded	sem chumbo	*saim shoomboo*
urgent	urgente	*oorgent*
urgently	urgentemente	*oorgentment*
urine	urina	*ooreena*
usually	geralmente	*gerarlment*

V

vacate	desocupar	*dezocoopar*
vaccinate	vacinar	*vasseenar*
vagina	vagina	*vajeena*
vaginal infection	infecção vaginal	*eenfecksow vajeenal*
valid	válido	*valleedoo*
valley	vale	*val*
valuable	valioso	*vallyoezoo*
van	carrinha	*careenya*
vanilla	baunilha	*bowneelya*
vase	jarra	*jahra*
vaseline	vaselina	*vasseleena*
veal	carne de vitela	*carn duh veetela*
vegetable soup	sopa de legumes	*soppa duh legoomesh*
vegetables	legumes	*legoomesh*
vegetarian	vegetariano	*vejetaryarnoo*
vein	veia	*veya*
venereal disease	doença venérea	*dooensa venerria*
via	através de	*atravej duh*
video camera	cámara de vídeo	*camara duh veedyoo*
video recorder	gravador de vídeo	*gravvadoor duh veedyoo*
video tape	cassette de vídeo	*casset duh veedyoo*
view	vista	*veeshta*
village	aldeia	*aldaya*
visa	visto	*veeshtoo*
visit	visita	*vizeeta*
vitamin tablets	vitaminas em comprimido	*veetameenash aim compreemeedoo*
vitamin	vitamina	*veetameena*
volcano	vulcão	*voolcow*
volleyball, to play	jogar voleibol	*joogar volaybol*
vomit	vomitar	*voomeetar*

W

wait	esperar	*eshperar*
waiter	empregado/garçom	*empregardoo/garsoom*

English	Portuguese	Pronunciation
waiting room	sala de espera	*sarla di eshpaira*
waitress	empregada	*empregarda*
wake up	despertar	*deshpairtar*
Wales	Gales	*garlesh*
walk	passeio	*passayoo*
walk	passear	*passayar*
walk	andar	*andar*
wallet	carteira	*cartayra*
wardrobe	guardaroupa	*gwarda roepa*
warm, heat	calor	*calor*
warn	avisar	*aveezar*
warning	aviso	*aveezoo*
wash	lavar	*lavar*
washing	roupa	*roepa*
washing line	corda de estender roupa	*corda di eshtendair roepa*
washing machine	máquina de lavar	*markeena duh lavar*
washing powder	sabão em pó	*sabow aim poh*
wasp	vespa	*veshpa*
watch, clock	relógio	*relogyoo*
water	água	*agwa*
waterfall	queda d'água	*kayda di agwa*
water ski	esqui aquático	*eshkee akwateecoo*
waterproof	impermeável	*eempairmeearvel*
wavepool	jacuzzi	*jacoozi*
way	lado/direcção	*lardoo (deeressow)*
we	nós	*noj*
weak	fraco	*frarcoo*
weather	tempo	*tempoo*
weather forecast	boletim meteorológico	*boleteem metrolojeecoo*
wedding	casamento	*cazzamentoo*
Wednesday	quarta-feira	*cwarta fayra*
week	semana	*semarna*
weekend	fim de semana	*feem duh semarna*
weekend duty	serviço de fim de semana	*sairveesoo duh feem duh semarna*
weekly ticket	passe semanal	*pass semarnal*
welcome	bem vindo	*baim veendoo*
well cooked	bem passado	*baim passardoo*
well, good	bom/bem	*bom/baim*
west	oeste	*wesht*
wet	húmido	*oomeedoo*
wet (weather)	chuvoso	*shoovozoo*
wetsuit	fato de surfe	*fartoo duh surf*
what?	o quê?	*oo kay?*
wheel	roda	*rodda*
wheelchair	cadeira de rodas	*cadayra duh roddash*
when?	quando?	*cwarndoo*
where?	onde?	*ond*
which?	qual?	*cwarl*
whipped cream	chantilly	*shanteelee*
white	branco	*brancoo*
white kidney beans	feijão branco	*fayjow brancoo*
who?	quem?	*kaim*
wholemeal	integral	*eentegral*
wholemeal bread	pão integral	*pow eentegral*

why?	porquê?	*porkay?*
wide-angle lens	objectiva de grande abertura	*objeteeva duh grand abairtoora*
widow	viúva	*veeoova*
widower	viúvo	*veeoovoo*
wife	mulher/esposa	*moolyair/eshpoza*
wind	vento	*ventoo*
windbreak	páravento	*parra ventoo*
windmill	moinho	*mooeenyoo*
window	janela	*janella*
windscreen wiper	limpa pára-brisas	*leempa parra-breezash*
wine	vinho	*veenyoo*
wine list	lista de vinhos	*leeshta duh veenyoosh*
wine shop	casa de vinhos	*carza duh veenyoosh*
winter	inverno	*eenvairnoo*
witness	testemunha	*teshtemoonya*
woman	mulher	*moolyair*
wood	madeira	*madayra*
wool	lã	*lar*
word	palavra	*palavra*
work	trabalho	*trabalyoo*
working day	dia útil	*deeah ooteel*
worn	usado	*oosardoo*
worried	preocupado	*preeoccupardoo*
wound	ferida	*fereeda*
wrap	embrulhar	*aimbroolyar*
wrist	pulso	*poolsoo*
write	escrever	*eshcrevair*
writing pad	bloco	*blohkoo*
(squared, lined)	(quadrado, pautado)	*(qwardrardoo, powtardoo)*
written	por escrito	*por shcreetoo*
wrong	errado	*errardoo*

Y

yacht	iate	*yat*
year	ano	*arnoo*
yellow	amarelo	*amarelloo*
yes	sim	*si*
yes, please	sim, se faz favor	*si, suh faj favvor*
yesterday	ontem	*ontaim*
yoghurt	iogurte	*yogoort*
you (polite)	o senhor	*oo senyor*
you	você	*vossay*
you too	igualmente	*eegwalment*
youth hostel	albergue de juventude	*albairg duh jooventood*

Z

zip	fecho de correr	*feshoo duh coorair*
zoo	jardim zoológico	*jardeem zoo-oloojeecoo*

Basic grammar

1. Definite and indefinite articles – **the** and **a**

Apart from verbs and adverbs, words in Portuguese are either masculine or feminine with **o** or **a** being the definite article and **um** or **uma** the indefinite article:

	Singular	Plural	
Masculine	*o*	*os*	- the
Feminine	*a*	*as*	- the
Masculine	*um*	*uns*	- some
Feminine	*uma*	*umas*	- some

e.g. *um homem/uns homens* (a man/some men)

The definite/indefinite article, the noun, verb and adjectives all correspond to each other in terms of number and gender,
e.g. *O homem cansado entrou no banco* (The tired man went into the bank)

2. Plural

Adding an **s** is usually sufficient:
> *casa/casas*   (house/houses)

Some nouns form the plural irregularly, such as:

cão > cães	(dog/s)
relação > relações	(relationship/s)
mão > mãos	(hand/s)
doutor > doutores	(doctor/s)
canal > canais	(channel/s)
hotel > hotéis	(hotel/s)
lençol > lençóis	(sheet/s)

3. Personal pronouns

In general *tu* is used for **you** when speaking to close friends, relations and children and pets; *o senhor/a senhora* (or *você*) is used in all other cases:

eu	I
tu	you (familiar)
você	you (semi familiar)
o senhora/a senhora	you (polite)
ele/ela	he/she
nós	we
vós	you (familar)
vocês	you (semi familar)
os senhores/as senhoras	you (polite)
eles/elas	they

4. Possessive pronouns

These correspond to the object they modify:

o meu/a minha	(my)	*o meu amigo* (my friend)
os meus/as minhas	(my)	*os meus amigos* (my friends)
o teu/a tua	(your)	*o teu irmão* (your brother)
os teus/as tuas	(your)	*os teus irmãos* (your brothers)

o seu/a sua	(your/his)	*o seu marido* (your/his/her/her husband)
os seus/as suas	(your)	*os seus filhos* (your/their sons)/their)
dele	(his)	*a casa dele* (his house)
dela	(her)	*o carro dela* (her car)
deles/delas	(their)	*o neto deles/delas* (their grandson)
o nosso/a nossa	(our)	*o nosso cão* (our dog)
os nossos/as nossas	(our)	*os nossos gatos* (our cats)
o vosso/a vossa	(your)	*o vosso pai* (your father)
os vossos/as vossas	(your)	*os vossos tios* (your uncles)

5. Verbs

The most widely used tenses are the present, past and future, and the three main verb groups are those ending in -*ar*, -*er* and -*ir*, e.g.

falar	(to speak)	
eu	(I)	*falo*
tu	(you)	*falas*
ele/ela	(he/she)	*fala*
você	(you)	*fala*
o(a) senhor(a)	(you)	*fala*
nós	(we)	*falamos*
vocês	(you)	*falam*
as senhoras	(they)	*falam*
os senhores	(they)	*falam*
eles/elas	(they)	*falam*

Portuguese has two different verbs of being, *ser* and *estar*, applying to permanent and temporary states respectively.

ser	(to be)
eu sou	(I am)
tu es	(you are)
ele/ela é	(he/she is)
você é	(you are)
o(a) senhor(a) é	(you are)
nós somos	(we are)
vocês são	(you are)
as senhoras são	(they are)
os senhores são	(they are)
eles/elas são	(they are)

e.g. *O meu pai é médico* (My father <u>is</u> a doctor)

estar	(to be)
eu estou	(I am)
tu estás	(you are)
ele/ela está	(he/she is)
você está	(you are)
o(a) senhor(a) está	(you are)
nós estamos	(we are)
vocês estão	(you are)
as senhores estão	(they are)
os senhores estão	(they are)
eles/elas estão	(they are)

e.g. *A comida está quente* (The food <u>is</u> hot).

6. Demonstrative pronouns

este/esta this (describes a noun, e.g. **_Este livro_** This book)
isto this (used alone e.g. **_O que é isto?_** What is this?)
_esse/essa_that
aquele/aquela that (more distant)

7. Negatives

In order to form a negative sentence, **_não_** is placed before the verb, e.g. **_Não falo_** (I don't speak).

Other negative forms:
ninguém nobody
nenhum(a) none
nem...nem neither...nor
nada nothing
nunca never